Festive Entertaining

GENERAL EDITOR
CHUCK WILLIAMS

RECIPES
JOYCE GOLDSTEIN AND OTHER CONTRIBUTORS

PHOTOGRAPHY
ALLAN ROSENBERG AND ALLEN V. LOTT

TIME
LIFE
BOOKS

TIME-LIFE BOOKS
Time-Life Books is a division of Time Life Inc.
Time-Life is a trademark of Time Warner Inc. U.S.A.

Time-Life Custom Publishing
Vice President and Publisher: Terry Newell
Managing Editor: Donia Ann Steele
Director of Acquisitions: Jennifer L. Pearce
Vice President of Sales and Marketing: Neil Levin
Director of Financial Operations: J. Brian Birky

WILLIAMS-SONOMA
Founder and Vice-Chairman: Chuck Williams
Book Buyer: Victoria Kalish

WELDON OWEN INC.
President: John Owen
Vice President and Publisher: Wendely Harvey
Chief Operating Officer: Larry Partington
Vice President International Sales: Stuart Laurence
Managing Editor: Val Cipollone
Consulting Editors: Norman Kolpas, Judith Dunham
Copy Editor: Sharon Silva
Design: John Bull, The Book Design Company
Production Director: Stephanie Sherman
Production Consultant: Sarah Lemas
Production Manager: Jen Dalton
Production Editor: Deborah Cowder
Food Photographer: Allan Rosenberg
Additional Photography: Allen V. Lott
Food Stylists: Heidi Gintner, Susan Massey,
   John Phillip Carroll, Peggy Fallon
Prop Stylist: Sandra Griswold
Illustrations: Alice Harth

The Williams-Sonoma Kitchen Library
conceived and produced by Weldon Owen Inc.
814 Montgomery St., San Francisco, CA 94133

In collaboration with Williams-Sonoma
3250 Van Ness Ave., San Francisco, CA 94109

Production by Toppan Printing Co., (HK) Ltd.
Printed in China

A Note on Weights and Measures:
All recipes include customary U.S. and metric
measurements. Metric conversions are based on
a standard developed for these books and have
been rounded off. Actual weights may vary.

A Weldon Owen Production

Copyright © 1998 Weldon Owen Inc.

Library of Congress
Cataloging-in-Publication Data:

Festive entertaining /general editor, Chuck Williams ; recipes, Joyce
    Goldstein . . . [et al.] ; photography, Allan Rosenberg and Allen
    V. Lott.
       p.   cm. — (Williams-Sonoma kitchen library)
    Includes index.
    ISBN 0-7370-2002-4
    1. Entertaining. I. Williams, Chuck.   II. Goldstein, Joyce
Esersky.   III. Series.
TX731.F48   1998
642.4—dc21   98-14973
                                                                  CIP

Contents

STARTERS 15

SALADS & SIDE DISHES 41

MAIN COURSES 61

DESSERTS 83

INTRODUCTION

So many of life's moments, big and small, are worthy of special celebration: a traditional holiday, a birthday or an anniversary, a homecoming. Such occasions become even more festive when recognized with good food, thoughtfully prepared and served.

Think back to the most memorable parties you've ever given or attended and you'll probably discover that one word applies to them all: *effortless*. Truly festive entertaining flows with an ease and style all its own. Of course, such events don't happen without planning and inspiration. From the first cause for celebration to the final cleanup, great parties depend equally upon organization and creativity. This book aims to provide you with both.

On the next few pages, you'll find strategies and information that will help you put together a party from the guest list to the menu to the table settings. Many of the 45 recipes that follow have been created by master chef and cookbook author Joyce Goldstein to be not only festive but also easy to prepare, with much of the work doable in advance. Most of the recipes work for everyday meals, too, and can be easily paired with old favorites. I hope you'll find among them new candidates for your permanent culinary repertoire.

Whether you use the recipes and suggestions in this book to throw a grand holiday feast or plan and cook a simple welcome-home dinner, the goal remains the same: to make the event as easy and enjoyable for you, the host or hostess, as it is for your guests.

Chuck Williams

Festive Entertaining Basics

The success of a party begins with the guest list. Indeed, deciding on a group of compatible people is as important as arriving at a suitable menu. The value of inviting guests with a fair bit in common and pairing them with a menu that allows you time spent away from the kitchen cannot be underestimated.

Being organized is important, too. A well-built menu is one that lets you ready some dishes in advance. The more you can do beforehand, the lighter your workload the day of the party. Many of the recipes in this book can be made ahead, and most of the ingredients they call for are widely available at well-stocked food stores or from a reliable butcher or fishmonger.

Setting the scene also counts. The dining room is the obvious place to start, but, depending upon the number of guests, the occasion, and the time of year, you could just as easily set a table for two by the fireside or dine al fresco. Once you settle on a venue, consider table dressings, floral arrangements, lighting, and music, all of which should underscore the theme of the party. There's no need, however, to go beyond what's practical. Work with what you have available and don't hesitate to mix and match. Two simple elements, fresh flowers and candlelight, can always be counted on for ambience.

Don't panic if something goes wrong. More likely than not, events that don't turn out exactly as you'd planned will go unnoticed. Remember that great parties develop lives of their own, so relax and have a good time.

Planning Menus

Let the occasion and the season be your first guides to the foods you might serve for a festive meal. Then leaf through the recipes in this book to begin planning your menu, choosing complementary starters, main courses, side dishes or salads, and desserts. The four menus given below only begin to suggest the possibilities.

❧ Spring Celebration ❧
Caesar Salad
Rack of Spring Lamb with Mediterranean Flavors
Asparagus and Potatoes with Almonds and Mint
Citrus and Honey Cheesecake with Nut Crust

❧ Pretheater Cocktails ❧
Greek Chicken Strudel
Roasted Peppers with Herbed Goat Cheese
Crab in Endive Leaves
Mushrooms Stuffed with Sweet Sausage

❧ Harvest Dinner ❧
Spiced Squash and Apple Soup
Roast Chicken with Herbs
Chanterelles, Chestnuts, and Pearl Onions
Mandarin Orange Custard Tart

❧ Al Fresco Lunch ❧
Grilled Figs with Goat Cheese in Grape Leaves
Grilled Shrimp with Charmoula
Green Salad
Warm Blueberry Shortcakes

Setting the Table

The choices you make in setting your table with dishes, napkins, and centerpieces play an important role in establishing the style of your party. Shown here is a classic option for each. The spirit of simplicity behind them applies to any festive occasion.

Ideally, dishes should flatter the food you serve on them. More practically, work with what you have, mixing and matching patterns and borrowing or renting if necessary. In the setting below, fine china is complemented by silver flatware, a linen napkin, and cut-crystal glasses. Each item is carefully positioned in order of use. Glassware is arranged with similar logic. Closest to the right hand is a glass for white wine. To its left, a larger glass awaits red wine. Above both glasses is a water goblet. Dessert utensils may be set out beforehand, as shown. Alternatively, place them beside the dessert plates at serving time.

The simple Astoria napkin fold shown on the opposite page achieves a graceful effect suitable for both elegant and informal settings. For clarity, the illustration uses a plain 20-inch-square (50-cm) linen napkin. Feel free to use any napkins you like.

Finally, when preparing or buying centerpieces such as the festive arrangement shown, remember that flowers to be kept on the table during the meal are best low and spread out, allowing guests to see one another across the table.

Folding Napkins

The simple Astoria fold is well suited to both informal and elegant settings.

1. Fold the napkin into quarters by first folding down the top half, then folding the left side over the right.

2. Rotate 90 degrees so the open end points toward you. Fold the top point down to the center.

3. Fold in the left corner so its point reaches just past the center.

4. Cross the right corner just over the left and carefully turn the napkin over.

Rose Braid

Roses can be counted on to make festive arrangements. For one that is really special, try this rose braid.

You'll need about five dozen roses in all. The open petals of garden roses give a fuller look; if you plan to use hothouse roses, buy them two days ahead of time so they can open a bit. An urn-shaped vase provides height to lift the braid. Cut a piece of florist's foam to fit the container and soak it in warm water for 30 minutes; place it inside the vase and add water. Arrange about three dozen of the roses, ends trimmed, in a bouquet shape and fill any gaps with small roses or tight buds.

For the braid, you'll need florist's tape and thin wire. Select about 12 roses, in an even range of blossom sizes from small to large. Trim all their stems to a uniform 6-inch (15-cm) length. As a base for the braid, use two 18-inch-long (45-cm) strands of variegated ivy.

1. Begin braiding.
Hold the two 18-inch-long (45-cm) strands of ivy parallel to each other. At one end, attach three small, partially opened roses with 6-inch (15-cm) stems, wrapping florist's wire around the stems and ivy. Trim the rose stems to 1 inch (2.5 cm) past the wire.

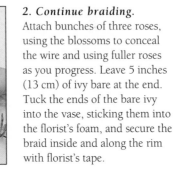

2. Continue braiding.
Attach bunches of three roses, using the blossoms to conceal the wire and using fuller roses as you progress. Leave 5 inches (13 cm) of ivy bare at the end. Tuck the ends of the bare ivy into the vase, sticking them into the florist's foam, and secure the braid inside and along the rim with florist's tape.

Carving a chicken properly is easy and makes for an attractive presentation. Use a sturdy two-pronged fork to steady the chicken as you carve it with a sharp knife. The breast can be removed in several slices or in one piece.

1. Remove the leg and the wing.
Cut through the skin between the leg and breast to locate the thigh joint; cut through the joint to sever the leg (shown at left). Cut through the shoulder joint where it meets the breast to remove the wing.

2. Separate the drumstick and thigh.
If the chicken is small, serve the whole leg as one portion. If it is large, cut through the joint to separate the drumstick and thigh into two pieces.

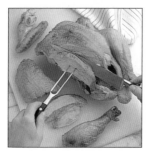

3. Carve the breast.
Starting at the breastbone, cut downward and parallel to the rib cage, carving the meat into long, thin slices. Or, cut the meat away from the breastbone in one piece.

Chicken Stock

Homemade chicken stock can be stored in tightly covered containers in the refrigerator for up to 2 days or in the freezer for up to 2 months.

6 lb (3 kg) stewing chicken parts
1 leek, including tender green tops, cut into 1-inch (2.5-cm) lengths
1 large yellow onion, unpeeled, root trimmed
1 large carrot, peeled and cut into 1-inch (2.5-cm) lengths
1 celery stalk with leaves, cut into 1-inch (2.5-cm) chunks
6 fresh parsley sprigs
3 fresh thyme sprigs
1 bay leaf
½ teaspoon peppercorns
5 qt (5 l) water

*I*n a large stockpot, combine the chicken, leek, onion, carrot, and celery. Wrap the parsley, thyme, bay leaf, and peppercorns in a square of cheesecloth (muslin) and tie securely with kitchen string. Add to the stockpot along with the water.

Place over medium-low heat and bring slowly to a simmer, skimming off any foam that rises to the surface. Cover partially and continue to simmer gently for about 2 hours, skimming occasionally.

Line a fine-mesh sieve or colander with a double thickness of cheesecloth and place over a large bowl. Remove the stock from the heat and pour through the sieve or colander; discard the solids. Place the stock, uncovered, in the refrigerator until completely cool. Lift off the fat that has solidified on top and discard. Store the stock as directed in the note.

Makes about 4 qt (4 l)

Beef Stock

Incomparably rich and deep in color, this stock will add an intense depth of flavor to the dishes on your entertaining menu. It takes all day to simmer, but you don't have to hover over the stove while it's cooking.

6 lb (3 kg) meaty beef shanks

2½ qt (2.5 l) cold water

beef scraps or other trimmings (optional)

2 yellow onions, coarsely chopped

1 leek, including tender green tops, coarsely chopped

2 carrots, peeled and coarsely chopped

1 celery stalk, coarsely chopped

about 1 cup (8 fl oz/250 ml) hot water

mushroom stems (optional)

6 cloves garlic

4 fresh parsley sprigs

3 fresh thyme sprigs

2 small bay leaves

10 whole peppercorns

Preheat an oven to 450°F (230°C). Place the beef shanks in a large roasting pan and roast, turning occasionally, until browned, about 1½ hours. Using tongs, transfer the shanks to a large stockpot and add the cold water and the beef scraps, if using; set the unwashed roasting pan aside. Bring to a boil over medium heat and skim off any foam that rises to the surface. Reduce the heat to low and cook uncovered, adding water as needed to keep the bones submerged. Skim the surface occasionally.

Meanwhile, place the roasting pan on the stove top. Add the onions, leek, carrots, and celery to the juices in the pan. Cook over high heat, stirring often, until the vegetables are browned, about 20 minutes. Add the vegetables to the stockpot. Pour the hot water into the roasting pan, bring to a simmer, and deglaze the pan, stirring with a wooden spoon to remove any browned bits from the bottom. Add to the stockpot.

Wrap the optional mushroom stems (if using), garlic, parsley sprigs, thyme sprigs, bay leaves, and peppercorns in a square of cheesecloth (muslin) and tie securely with kitchen string. Add to the stockpot. Simmer, uncovered, over low heat, for at least 6–8 hours, or preferably all day.

Line a fine-mesh sieve or colander with a double thickness of cheesecloth and place over a bowl. Remove the stock from the heat and pour through the sieve or colander; discard the solids. Place the stock in the refrigerator until completely cool. Lift off the fat that has solidified on top and discard. Store the stock in tightly covered containers in the refrigerator for up to 2 days or in the freezer for up to 2 months.

Makes about 2½ qt (2.5 l)

Tart Pastry

This classic pastry forms the foundation for all manner of savory tarts. The dough should be made at least 3 hours ahead, or preferably the night before, so it has time to chill. It may be stored in a plastic bag for up to 4 days in the refrigerator or for up to 2 months in the freezer.

1½ cups (7½ oz/235 g) all-purpose (plain) flour
2 pinches of salt
6 tablespoons (3 oz/90 g) unsalted butter, at room
   temperature, cut into rough chunks
1 small egg

To make the dough in a food processor, put the flour and salt into the work bowl and pulse a few times to mix. Add the butter and egg and pulse briefly just until the mixture comes together in a ball.

To make the dough by hand, place the flour, salt, and butter in a large bowl. Using your fingertips, mix the ingredients together until the butter is broken into large flakes coated with flour. Add the egg and continue to mix until the ingredients are the consistency of coarse crumbs. Gather the dough into a ball.

Put the ball of dough into a plastic bag and let it rest in the refrigerator for at least 3 hours before using. Remove the dough from the refrigerator about 30 minutes before rolling it out.

Makes 11 oz (345 g) dough

1. Combining the ingredients. Put the flour and salt in the bowl of a food processor; pulse a few times to combine. Add the chunks of butter and break in the egg.

2. Mixing the dough. Pulse the machine until the ingredients resemble coarse, moist crumbs, stopping several times to scrape the bowl as necessary. Process continuously just until the dough forms a ball that rides around the bowl on the blade.

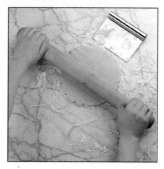

3. Rolling out the dough. Roll out on a lightly floured work surface, working from the center outward and giving the dough a quarter turn after each roll, until the thickness specified in individual recipes.

Basic Pie Pastry

This pastry can be used for sweet and savory pies. For a sweet crust, add the sugar; for a savory crust, leave it out. To achieve a flaky texture, make it with butter; for tender crusts, use vegetable shortening, or use half of each.

½ cup (4 oz/125 g) chilled unsalted butter or vegetable shortening (vegetable lard), or half of each
1½ cups (7½ oz/235 g) all-purpose (plain) flour
1 tablespoon sugar
½ teaspoon salt
3–4 tablespoons cold water

To make the dough by hand, cut the butter and/or shortening into small bits. Combine the flour, sugar, and salt in a bowl. Add the butter and/or shortening. With your fingertips, 2 knives, or a pastry blender, quickly blend the ingredients together until the mixture resembles coarse crumbs. Sprinkle on the water 1 table-spoon at a time, stirring and tossing with a fork after each addition. Add just enough water for the dough to come together in a rough mass.

To make the dough in a food processor, cut the butter and/or shortening into large pieces. Place the flour, sugar, salt, and butter and/or shortening in the work bowl. Process with rapid on-off pulses until the mixture resembles cornmeal; do not overprocess or the pastry will be tough. Add the water, a little at a time, and process until blended; do not let the mixture form a ball. Stop and feel the dough (take care not to touch the blade); it should be just damp enough to mass together. If necessary, add more water by teaspoonfuls, processing for just an instant after each addition.

For a Fully Baked Pie Shell

1. Line the shell.
Preheat an oven to 400°F (200°C). Prick the pie shell with the tines of a fork. Line with aluminum foil and fill with dried beans or pie weights.

2. Bake the shell.
Bake for 10 minutes, then lower the heat to 350°F (180°C) and bake until the shell is golden brown, 15–20 minutes longer. Remove the weights and aluminum foil during the last 5 minutes of baking. Let cool completely on a rack.

To roll out the dough, turn it out onto a lightly floured board. Using floured hands, pat the dough into a smooth cake. Roll out the dough and transfer it to the pan as directed in the recipe. Put the pie shell in the freezer and let it rest for at least 30 minutes before baking.

Makes 12 oz (375g) dough

Stuffed Cherry Tomatoes

36 cherry tomatoes, about 1½ oz
   (45 g) each

FOR THE OLIVE STUFFING:
6 boned and skinned canned sardines
   in olive oil, well drained and tails
   discarded
3 tablespoons black olive paste
1 tablespoon chopped celery leaves
3 gherkins, finely chopped
¼ teaspoon cayenne pepper

FOR THE CHEESE STUFFING:
¾ lb (375 g) fresh goat cheese, or ricotta
   cheese, drained
2 tablespoons extra-virgin olive oil
2 green (spring) onions, including the
   green portions, finely chopped
1 tablespoon minced fresh summer
   savory or parsley
ground black pepper to taste

Two different stuffings—one made with black olives, the other with creamy goat cheese—add variety of flavor and color to these festive summertime hors d'oeuvres. For an even more colorful presentation, look for yellow or orange cherry tomatoes. The fillings can be scooped into or served as dips for other vegetables, such as celery sticks or wedges of bell pepper (capsicum) as well.

Cut a small cap from the top of each tomato. Using a small spoon, scoop out the flesh (reserve for another use). Invert the hollowed-out tomatoes on a plate to drain.

To make the olive stuffing, place the sardines in a bowl and mash them with a fork. Add the olive paste, celery leaves, gherkins, and cayenne pepper and mix well. Fill 18 of the tomatoes with this stuffing.

To make the cheese stuffing, place the cheese in a bowl and mash it with a fork. Add the olive oil, green onions, summer savory or parsley, and black pepper. Mix well. Fill the remaining 18 tomatoes with this stuffing.

Serve the tomatoes cold.

Serves 6–8

Mushrooms Stuffed with Sweet Sausage

24 large white mushrooms

4 tablespoons (2 fl oz/60 ml) olive oil

½ cup (2 oz/60 g) chopped yellow onion

1 tablespoon minced garlic

½ lb (250 g) ground (minced) pork

½ teaspoon ground cinnamon

¼ teaspoon ground nutmeg

1 teaspoon toasted fennel seeds (*see glossary, page 107*)

1 tablespoon grated orange zest

¼ cup (1 oz/30 g) fine dried bread crumbs

salt and ground pepper to taste

1 cup (8 fl oz/250 ml) Chicken Stock (*page 10*) or broth

Whether passed as an hors d'oeuvre or plated as an appetizer, stuffed mushrooms are a classic prelude to an evening of feasting.

✠

Remove the stems from the mushrooms and chop; reserve the caps. In a large frying pan over medium heat, warm 2 tablespoons of the olive oil. Add the chopped onion and sauté until soft, about 5 minutes. Raise the heat to high, add the chopped mushroom stems, and cook until they start to become dry, about 5 minutes. Stir in the garlic and sauté until fragrant, about 1 minute. Transfer to a bowl and set aside.

Preheat an oven to 350°F (180°C).

Heat the remaining 2 tablespoons oil in the same pan. Add the pork, breaking it up with a fork, and cook, stirring often, until it is no longer pink, about 5 minutes. Stir in the cinnamon, nutmeg, fennel seeds, and orange zest. Add the mushroom-onion mixture and the bread crumbs; mix well. Season with salt and pepper and taste and adjust the rest of the spices. Remove from the heat and let cool slightly.

Stuff the pork mixture into the mushroom caps, dividing it evenly. Arrange the mushrooms in a baking pan, filling side up. Drizzle the stock or broth around them.

Bake until the filling is piping hot and the mushrooms are tender when pierced, 20–25 minutes. Serve warm.

Serves 8

Roasted Peppers with Herbed Goat Cheese

10 oz (315 g) fresh mild goat cheese,
   crumbled
2 tablespoons chopped fresh chives, plus
   whole chives for garnish (optional)
2 tablespoons chopped fresh parsley
1½ tablespoons chopped fresh basil
1 clove garlic, minced
1 teaspoon chopped fresh thyme
grated zest of ½ lemon
¼ teaspoon ground black pepper
pinch of cayenne pepper
heavy (double) cream, if needed
3 large red bell peppers (capsicums),
   roasted and peeled (*see glossary,
   page 104*), being careful not to tear
   the halves

*This simple hors d'oeuvre combines the rich, creamy tang of goat cheese
with the sweetness of bell peppers. Serve at the start of a special
Mediterranean-style meal.*

In a bowl, stir together the cheese, chives, parsley, basil, garlic,
chopped thyme, lemon zest, black pepper, and cayenne pepper.
Add a bit of cream if the mixture is very stiff and difficult to mix.

Dividing it evenly, spread the cheese mixture on the cut sides of
the pepper halves. Starting from a long side, roll them up into
cylinders. Place seam side down on a plate, cover, and refrigerate
for a few hours to firm the filling.

At serving time, cut each pepper roll crosswise into about
6 rounds. Arrange on a platter, garnish with the fresh chives, if
using, and serve.

Serves 6–8

Smoked Salmon Mousse

14 oz (440 g) smoked salmon
½ cup (4 oz/125 g) plain yogurt
½ teaspoon paprika
¼–½ teaspoon cayenne pepper
2 tablespoons extra-virgin olive oil
1 lemon

This savory mousse is light in flavor and consistency. It may be prepared up to 24 hours in advance and stored in the refrigerator. Serve with cucumber and thinly sliced rye bread, blini, or sticks of raw vegetables, adding a touch of elegance to any meal.

✠

Roughly chop half of the smoked salmon and place in a food processor. Add the yogurt, paprika, cayenne, and olive oil. Grate the zest of the lemon into the processor, then halve the lemon, squeeze it, and measure 2 tablespoons juice. Add the juice and process to form a thin purée.

Transfer the purée to a bowl. Coarsely chop the remaining salmon and add to the purée. Stir to mix well, cover, and refrigerate until serving.

Serves 8

Sesame Shrimp

24 large shrimp (prawns) in the shell
2 egg whites
3 tablespoons sesame seeds
peanut oil or vegetable oil for deep-frying

One of the most elegant of cocktail party treats, fried butterflied shrimp get a crisp, rich coating of sesame seeds—a Chinese-inspired treatment. You can coat and cook thin strips of boned and skinned chicken breast in the same way.

✠

Peel the shrimp, leaving the last shell segment with the tail fin intact. Using a sharp knife, slit each shrimp along the outside curve of the body, cutting three-fourths of the way through. Remove and discard the dark veinlike intestinal tract. Then flatten the shrimp with your hand, opening it out into a V-shape.

In a bowl, using a fork, beat the egg whites until frothy. Put the sesame seeds in another bowl.

Pour the oil into a deep-fat fryer or heavy saucepan to a depth of about 2 inches (5 cm). Place over medium heat and heat to 350°F (180°C), or until a small bit of bread tossed into the oil surfaces immediately. When the oil is ready, dip the shrimp first into the egg white, and then roll them in the sesame seeds. Working in batches, slip the shrimp into the hot oil, being careful not to crowd the pan, and cook, turning them with a slotted spoon, until golden brown, 2–3 minutes. Using the slotted spoon, transfer to paper towels to drain. Repeat until all the shrimp are cooked.

Arrange the shrimp on a serving platter or individual plates and serve hot, warm, or at room temperature.

Serves 6

Crab in Endive Leaves

grated zest of 1 lemon

2 tablespoons lemon juice

2 tablespoons chopped fresh chives

2 tablespoons chopped fresh parsley

1 teaspoon chopped fresh tarragon

½ cup (4 fl oz/125 ml) mayonnaise, or as
needed to bind

1 tablespoon Dijon mustard

1 lb (500 g) fresh-cooked crabmeat,
picked over for shell fragments
and flaked

¾ cup (4 oz/125 g) diced celery

salt, ground black pepper, and cayenne
pepper to taste

24 Belgian endive (chicory/witloof)
leaves

The crisp, slightly bitter endive contrasts nicely with the mild sweetness of the crab in this easy and elegant hors d'oeuvre.

✠

In a bowl, combine the lemon zest, lemon juice, chives, parsley, tarragon, mayonnaise, and mustard; mix well. Stir in the crab and celery and season with salt, black pepper, and cayenne. Cover and refrigerate up to 6 hours.

To serve, spoon the crab mixture into the endive leaves, dividing it evenly. Arrange on a platter, cover, and refrigerate for at least 30 minutes or up to 2 hours to firm the filling, then serve chilled.

Serves 8

Blue Cheese Tartlets

Tart Pastry (*page 12*) or purchased puff
    pastry
3 oz (90 g) spinach or Swiss chard, stems
    removed
1 egg
⅔ cup (5 fl oz/160 ml) heavy (double)
    cream
¾ cup (3 oz/90 g) finely shredded
    Emmentaler cheese
¼ teaspoon ground nutmeg
salt and ground pepper to taste
3 oz (90 g) Roquefort or other blue
    cheese, crumbled
2 tablespoons pine nuts

*The robust flavor of spinach or Swiss chard is a suitable match for the
tang of blue cheese. These bite-sized tarts are perfect to serve at a
cocktail party or before a special holiday meal.*

If using the tart pastry, prepare the dough as directed and
refrigerate for 3 hours. Remove from the refrigerator 30 minutes
before you are ready to roll it out. If using frozen puff pastry,
defrost in the refrigerator.

Preheat an oven to 425°F (220°C).

Bring a large saucepan three-fourths full of water to a boil.
Plunge the spinach or Swiss chard into the boiling water and
cook for 30 seconds. Immediately drain in a colander and rinse
with cold water to halt the cooking. Drain again, pressing against
the greens to force out as much water as possible, then chop
coarsely; set aside.

In a bowl, combine the egg, cream, Emmentaler cheese, and
nutmeg. Season with salt and pepper and beat with a fork until
well blended. Add the spinach or chard and stir well.

On a lightly floured board, roll out the dough as thinly as
possible. Using a fluted pastry cutter about 1¼ inches (3 cm) in
diameter, cut out 18 dough rounds. Use the rounds to line 18
individual tartlet pans or the wells in tartlet trays or miniature
muffin pans, pressing the dough gently in place. If using the
former, arrange the lined pans on a large baking sheet. Divide
the blue cheese evenly among the tartlets. Fill each with an
equal amount of the egg mixture. Scatter the pine nuts on top,
dividing equally.

Bake until the filling sets and the crust is golden, about
15 minutes. Transfer to a rack to cool briefly, then serve warm.

Serves 6

Greek Chicken Strudel

For the filling:

about 3 cups (24 fl oz/750 ml) Chicken
    Stock (*page 10*) or broth
6 boneless, skinless chicken breast halves
6 cups (12 oz/375 g) loosely packed
    chopped spinach leaves
3 tablespoons olive oil
1½ cups (5 oz/155 g) minced green
    (spring) onions, including tender
    green tops
⅓ cup (½ oz/15 g) chopped fresh dill
⅓ cup (½ oz/15 g) chopped fresh parsley
¾ lb (375 g) feta cheese, crumbled
5 oz (155 g) Monterey jack cheese,
    shredded
3 eggs, lightly beaten
1 teaspoon ground coriander
½ teaspoon ground nutmeg
¼ teaspoon cayenne pepper
¾ cup (3 oz/90 g) chopped toasted
    walnuts (*see glossary, page 107*)
salt and ground black pepper to taste

12 sheets filo pastry, thawed in the
    refrigerator if frozen
⅓–½ cup (3–4 oz/90–125 g) unsalted
    butter, melted, for brushing

This recipe is excellent served with cocktails or as a light first course with dinner. If you prefer, you could layer the filo and filling in lasagne pans, then slice into wedges to serve.

To make the filling, in a wide frying pan, pour in enough stock to cover the chicken breasts and bring to a boil. Add the breasts, reduce the heat to low, and poach, uncovered, until the chicken is cooked through, 8–10 minutes. Using a slotted spoon, transfer the chicken to a cutting board and let cool. Chop the chicken and place it in a bowl. Reserve the stock for another recipe.

Place the spinach with the rinsing water still clinging to the leaves in the same pan over medium heat. Stir until wilted, about 3 minutes. Drain well, squeeze dry, and add to the chicken.

In the same pan over medium heat, warm the olive oil. Add the green onions and sauté until soft, about 5 minutes. Add to the chicken and spinach, along with the dill, parsley, feta cheese, jack cheese, eggs, coriander, nutmeg, cayenne, and walnuts. Stir until well combined. Season liberally with salt and black pepper.

Preheat an oven to 325°F (165°C). Have ready 2 ungreased baking sheets.

Lay a filo sheet on a work surface, keeping the other sheets covered with a damp kitchen towel. Brush with the melted butter. Top with 3 more sheets, brushing each one with butter. Then place a thin row of the chicken mixture along a long side, about ½ inch (12 mm) from the edge. Tuck in the ends and roll up. Place seam side down on a baking sheet. Repeat with the remaining filling and filo, forming 2 more rolls.

Bake until golden brown, 25–30 minutes. Remove from the oven and let stand for 10 minutes. Then, using a serrated knife, cut crosswise into slices 1 inch (2.5 cm) thick and serve hot.

Serves 8–10

Tomato Tart

Basic Pie Pastry (*page 13*)
3 large tomatoes, cut into slices ½ inch
  (12 mm) thick
salt to taste
2 tablespoons Dijon mustard
3 tablespoons chopped fresh mint
¼ lb (125 g) Gruyère or Emmentaler
  cheese, cut into 8 thin slices
2 eggs
1 cup (8 fl oz/250 ml) heavy (double)
  cream
ground pepper to taste

This French-style tart could be given an Italian flair by substituting basil for the mint and mozzarella for the Gruyère. Instead of offering it as a starter, cut big wedges and present it as a light main course for a festive luncheon.

✠

On a lightly floured work surface, roll out the pastry dough into a round about 12 inches (30 cm) in diameter. Carefully transfer to a 10-inch (25-cm) tart pan with a removable bottom or pie pan, pressing it gently into the bottom and sides. If using a tart pan, cut off the pastry even with the rim; if using a pie pan, turn under the overhang and flute the edge decoratively. Place in the freezer for 30 minutes.

Meanwhile, using your fingers, carefully push out the seeds and watery juices from the tomato slices. Sprinkle the sliced tomatoes with salt and place in a large colander to drain for 30 minutes.

Preheat an oven to 350°F (180°C).

Remove the tomatoes from the colander and pat them dry. Using a rubber spatula, spread the mustard evenly over the bottom of the pastry shell. Sprinkle with the chopped mint. Top evenly with the cheese, then place the tomato slices over the cheese. In a small bowl, beat together the eggs and cream until blended. Season with salt and pepper and pour over the tomatoes.

Bake until pale gold and the custard is set, about 30 minutes. Remove from the oven, let rest for 10 minutes, then slice into thin wedges and serve.

Serves 8–10

Duck Livers with Apple-Ginger Butter

about 6 tablespoons (3 oz/90 g) unsalted
  butter, at room temperature
1 small apple, peeled, cored, and finely
  chopped
1 piece fresh ginger, about 2 inches
  (5 cm), peeled and grated
2 tablespoons calvados or other apple
  brandy
salt and ground pepper to taste
12 large duck or chicken livers

Perfumed by the apples and ginger, ultra-rich duck livers make an unforgettable hors d'oeuvre for a special occasion.

✠

*I*f using wooden skewers, soak in water to cover for about
30 minutes, then drain. Preheat a broiler (griller).

In a small frying pan, melt 2 tablespoons of the butter. Add the apple and ginger and cook, stirring, until the apple is very soft, 10–15 minutes. Add the brandy and cook for 1–2 minutes longer. Transfer the mixture to a blender or food processor and purée.

Place about 3 tablespoons of the remaining butter in a bowl, add the apple purée, and, using a wooden spoon, mix together until thick and creamy. Add the remaining butter, if needed, to achieve the correct consistency. Season with salt and pepper. (The butter may be made up to 1 day ahead of time, covered, and brought to room temperature before serving.)

Trim the livers carefully of fat and sinew. Thread onto skewers, being careful not to crowd them so they will cook evenly, and sprinkle with salt and pepper. Place on a broiler pan and slip under the broiler about 4 inches (10 cm) from the heat source. Broil (grill), turning once, until browned on the outside and medium-rare in the center, about 2 minutes on each side.

Remove the livers from the skewers, place 2 on each plate, and top with the apple-ginger butter, dividing evenly. Serve at once.

Serves 6

Grilled Figs with Goat Cheese in Grape Leaves

6 bottled grape leaves, rinsed of brine
   and stemmed
6 slices mild fresh goat cheese, each
   about 1 inch (2.5 cm) thick
6 large, ripe figs
6 thin slices prosciutto
olive oil for brushing
ground pepper to taste
6 lime wedges

*Offer these at the start of a special lunch or dinner party, when figs are
in season. The goat cheese and grape leaf packages can be made the
night before serving, covered, and refrigerated.*

✠

*I*f using wooden skewers, soak 6 skewers in water to cover for
30 minutes, then drain.

Prepare a fire in a charcoal grill. Oil the grill rack and
position it 4–6 inches (10–15 cm) above the fire. Or preheat
a broiler (griller).

Place the grape leaves, shiny side down, on a work surface.
Wrap each slice of goat cheese in a leaf, folding in the ends and
sides to form a neat packet.

Cut each fig in half lengthwise. Cut the prosciutto slices in half
lengthwise. Wrap each fig half with a piece of prosciutto and
thread 2 halves onto each of 6 skewers. Brush the wrapped figs
and cheese packets lightly with olive oil and sprinkle with pepper.

Place the figs and cheese on the grill rack over medium-hot
coals or under the broiler about 4 inches (10 cm) from the heat
source. Grill or broil, turning once, until the figs are heated
through, about 3 minutes, and the cheese is soft and warm,
about 4 minutes.

Divide evenly among 6 small plates. Garnish each plate with
a lime wedge and serve at once.

Serves 6

Spiced Squash and Apple Soup

¼ cup (2 oz/60 g) unsalted butter or
   ¼ cup (2 fl oz/60 ml) olive oil
2 large yellow onions, chopped
2 large green apples, peeled, cored, and
   diced, plus thin slices for garnish
1 teaspoon ground nutmeg
½ teaspoon ground allspice
½ teaspoon ground cinnamon
10 cups (5 lb/2.5 kg) peeled, seeded,
   and diced butternut squash (about
   4 squashes)
3 qt (3 l) Chicken Stock (*page 10*)
   or broth
salt and ground pepper to taste

Golden in color and fragrant in spice, this soup is the perfect start to an autumn or a winter holiday dinner. Butternut squash is similar to pumpkin in taste and texture but is easier to peel and dice. Apple lightens and sweetens the purée.

✠

In a large pot over medium heat, melt the butter or warm the olive oil. Add the onions and diced apples and cook, stirring often, until tender, about 10 minutes. Stir in the nutmeg, allspice, and cinnamon and cook for about 1 minute. Then add the squash and the chicken stock or broth, raise the heat to medium-high, and bring to a boil. Reduce the heat to low and simmer, uncovered, until the squash is very tender, 20–30 minutes.

Remove from the heat and let cool slightly. Working in batches and using a slotted spoon, transfer the squash, apples, and onion with a little bit of the liquid to a blender or food processor and purée until smooth. Transfer to a clean saucepan. Add enough of the remaining liquid to make a medium-thick soup. (If not serving right away, reserve any leftover liquid, as the soup may thicken on standing.) Season with salt and pepper, then taste and adjust the spices. (This soup may be made up to 1 day ahead, refrigerated uncovered until cold, and then covered.)

Place the soup over medium-low heat and heat almost to scalding. Ladle into warmed bowls and top with thin apple slices. Serve immediately.

Serves 10–12

Beet, Cabbage, and Mushroom Borscht

8–10 large beets

3 tablespoons olive oil

2 large red (Spanish) onions, chopped

6 large carrots, peeled and sliced

2 heads green cabbage, cored and shredded

4 cups (12 oz/375 g) sliced white mushrooms

1 lemon, pricked with a fork in several places

2½ qt (2.5 l) Beef Stock (*page 11*) or broth or vegetable stock or broth

salt and ground pepper to taste

sugar to taste

lemon juice, if needed

½ cup (¾ oz/20 g) chopped fresh dill

This Eastern European soup tastes best if made the day before serving. Its ruby red color adds a festive air to the dinner table.

If the greens are still attached to the beets, trim them, leaving about 2 inches (5 cm) of each stem intact. (Reserve the greens for another use.) Place the unpeeled beets in a large saucepan with water to cover. Bring to a boil, then reduce the heat to low, and simmer, uncovered, until tender when pierced, 30–50 minutes; the timing will depend upon the size of the beets. Drain and, when cool enough to handle, slip off the skins and dice the beets. Set aside.

In a large, heavy pot over medium heat, warm the olive oil. Add the onions and carrots and cook, stirring occasionally, for about 10 minutes. Add the beets, cabbage, mushrooms, lemon, and stock or broth and bring to a boil. Reduce the heat to low and simmer, uncovered, until the soup is red and the flavors are blended, about 30 minutes. Remove the lemon and discard. Season with salt and pepper, then adjust the seasoning with sugar and lemon juice, if necessary.

Ladle into warmed bowls. Sprinkle with the dill, dividing it evenly, and serve at once.

Serves 10–12

Fennel, Pear, and Frisée Salad

FOR THE VINAIGRETTE:

6 tablespoons (3 fl oz/90 ml) white wine
    vinegar
1 tablespoon peeled and grated fresh
    ginger
¾ teaspoon sugar
¾ cup (6 fl oz/180 ml) olive oil
salt and ground pepper to taste

FOR THE SALAD:

1 medium head frisée or 2 bunches
    watercress
2 small fennel bulbs
2 firm but ripe Comice or other
    winter pears

This salad is a wonderful fresh-tasting complement to roast poultry. You can assemble the fennel and greens up to 30 minutes ahead, but slice the pears and dress the salad just before serving.

To make the vinaigrette, in a small bowl, stir together the vinegar and grated ginger. Let stand for 5 minutes, then whisk in the sugar and the oil to make a vinaigrette. Season with salt and pepper.

To make the salad, trim the tough stems from the frisée or watercress and place in a bowl. Cut off the stems and feathery tops and any bruised outer stalks from the fennel bulbs; reserve any attractive tops for garnish, if you like. Cut the bulbs lengthwise into quarters and remove the hard center core. Thinly slice crosswise. Cut the pears in half lengthwise, remove the stems, cores, and seeds, then thinly slice.

Drizzle half of the vinaigrette over the frisée or watercress and toss to coat. Divide among 4 plates. Arrange the fennel and pear slices over the greens and drizzle the rest of the vinaigrette over the top. Garnish with the reserved fennel tops, if using. Serve immediately.

Serves 4

Caesar Salad

FOR THE CROUTONS:

18 baguette slices, each about ⅛ inch
   (3 mm) thick (about ½ loaf)
olive oil
1 or 2 cloves garlic, halved

FOR THE SALAD:

3 eggs
3–4 tablespoons finely chopped
   anchovy fillets
6 tablespoons (3 fl oz/90 ml) lemon juice
¾ cup (6 fl oz/180 ml) extra-virgin
   olive oil
1 tablespoon minced garlic
4–6 tablespoons (1–1½ oz/30–45 g)
   grated Parmesan cheese
ground pepper to taste
4–6 small heads romaine (cos) lettuce

After plain mixed greens, this is probably the most popular salad in the United States. If possible, use salt-packed anchovies, as they have better flavor. Lightly rinse off the excess salt and remove any small bones before chopping. The croutons can be made the night before.

⊕

*T*o make the croutons, preheat an oven to 350°F (180°C). Arrange the bread in a single layer on a baking sheet. Brush the tops of the slices with olive oil. Bake until crisp and golden, 8–10 minutes. Remove from the oven. While the bread slices are still warm, rub the tops with the cut sides of a garlic clove. Let cool.

To make the salad, bring a small saucepan three-fourths full of water to a boil. Working quickly, lower each egg on a spoon into the boiling water. Allow the eggs to remain in the water for 1 minute, then transfer to a bowl of cold water to cool completely.

In a bowl, mash the anchovies with the lemon juice. Break the eggs and add them to the bowl along with the olive oil, minced garlic, and 3 tablespoons of the Parmesan cheese. Whisk together until all the ingredients are fully incorporated. Season with pepper.

Tear the romaine leaves into large bite-sized pieces and place in a large salad bowl. Add the croutons and the dressing and toss to coat the leaves evenly.

Transfer to individual plates and sprinkle with the remaining Parmesan cheese to taste. Serve at once.

Serves 6

Avocado, Grapefruit, and Endive Salad

FOR THE VINAIGRETTE:

¼ cup (⅓ oz/10 g) lightly packed
   chopped fresh mint
¼ cup (2 fl oz/60 ml) lemon juice
½ cup (4 fl oz/125 ml) grapefruit juice
1 cup (8 fl oz/250 ml) olive oil
3 tablespoons honey
1 tablespoon grated grapefruit zest
salt and ground pepper to taste

FOR THE SALAD:

4 small heads Belgian endive
   (chicory/witloof), separated into leaves
   and thinly sliced lengthwise
1 cup (1 oz/30 g) fresh mint leaves, plus
   ¼ cup (⅓ oz/10 g) chopped fresh mint
3 pink grapefruits, peeled and cut into
   segments (see glossary, page 105)
3 ripe avocados, halved, pitted, peeled,
   and thinly sliced lengthwise

Serve this simple, refreshing salad as part of a weekend brunch or light, warm-weather dinner. Shop for the avocados a few days in advance to ensure they ripen in time.

To make the vinaigrette, in a small saucepan, combine the chopped mint and lemon juice and bring to a boil. Remove from the heat and let steep for 10 minutes. Strain into a bowl. Add the grapefruit juice, olive oil, honey, and grapefruit zest and whisk together until blended. Season with salt and pepper, then taste and adjust the sweet-tart ratio if necessary.

To make the salad, combine the endive leaves and whole mint leaves in a salad bowl. Drizzle with half of the vinaigrette and toss to coat. Place on a serving platter or divide among 6 individual plates. Alternate the grapefruit segments and avocado slices atop the greens. Drizzle with the remaining vinaigrette and top with the chopped mint. Serve immediately.

Serves 6

Lobster, Potato, and Green Bean Salad with Pesto Vinaigrette

3 live lobsters, 1–1¼ lb (500–625 g) each
ice water, as needed
12–18 small red new potatoes or Yellow
   Finn potatoes, about 2 lb (1 kg) total
   weight
1½ lb (750 g) green beans, trimmed and
   cut into 2-inch (5-cm) lengths
1 cup (1½ oz/45 g) tightly packed fresh
   basil leaves
1 teaspoon minced garlic
2 tablespoons toasted pine nuts or
   walnuts *(see glossary, page 107)*
about ¾ cup (6 fl oz/180 ml) olive oil
¼ cup (2 fl oz/60 ml) red wine vinegar
salt and ground pepper to taste
butter lettuce
cherry tomatoes

*B*ring a very large pot three-fourths full of salted water to a boil over high heat. Drop in the lobsters, immersing completely, cover, and cook for 10 minutes. Remove the lobsters from the pot and drop them into a sinkful of ice water. (If desired, refrigerate the lobsters overnight.) Cut each lobster in half lengthwise and remove the meat from the body and claws as directed on page 106. Discard the shells. Cut the meat into bite-sized pieces, place in a bowl, cover, and refrigerate until serving.

Place the potatoes in a saucepan with salted water to cover and bring to a boil over high heat. Reduce the heat to medium and simmer, uncovered, until the potatoes are cooked through but still firm, 10–20 minutes. Drain and refrigerate to halt the cooking.

Bring a large pot three-fourths full of salted water to a boil. Drop in the green beans and cook until tender-crisp, 2–4 minutes. Drain and plunge the beans into ice water to halt the cooking. Drain, pat dry, and set aside.

In a food processor or blender, combine the basil leaves, garlic, and nuts. Pulse to combine. Add about ½ cup (4 fl oz/125 ml) of the olive oil and process to form a coarse purée. Transfer to a bowl and stir in the vinegar and enough of the remaining oil to make a spoonable vinaigrette. Season with salt and pepper.

To serve, cut the potatoes into slices ¼ inch (6 mm) thick. In a large bowl, combine the potatoes and green beans with half the vinaigrette. Toss to coat. Line 6 individual plates with lettuce leaves. Divide the potato mixture among the plates, top with the lobster pieces, and drizzle with the remaining vinaigrette. Garnish with cherry tomatoes and serve immediately.

Serves 6

Spiced Lentils

2 cups (14 oz/440 g) green or brown
  lentils
1 bay leaf
1 teaspoon salt
½ cup (4 fl oz/125 ml) plus
  3 tablespoons olive oil
¼ cup (2 fl oz/60 ml) lemon juice
2 cups (8 oz/250 g) chopped yellow
  onions
1 teaspoon minced garlic
2 tablespoons ground cumin
1 teaspoon ground coriander
grated zest of 1 lemon
½ cup (¾ oz/20 g) chopped fresh mint
salt and ground pepper to taste

*An excellent side dish for grilled meats, this goes especially well with
lamb. For the best texture, make this dish no more than several hours
in advance. If you make it ahead, fold in half of the mint, then add the
rest just before serving.*

In a deep saucepan, combine the lentils and bay leaf. Add water
to cover by 3 inches (7.5 cm) and bring to a boil over high heat.
Add the salt, reduce the heat to low, cover, and simmer until the
lentils are tender but still firm. Green lentils can take as long as
45 minutes, while brown lentils can take as few as 15 minutes, so
keep testing. When the lentils are done, drain well and place in a
bowl. Add the ½ cup (4 fl oz/125 ml) olive oil and the lemon
juice, toss well, and set aside.

In a large frying pan over medium heat, warm the 3 tablespoons oil. Add the onions and sauté until tender and translucent,
about 10 minutes. Add the garlic, cumin, coriander, and lemon
zest and continue to sauté until the garlic is soft and the flavors
are blended, 2–3 minutes longer.

Add the cooked onion mixture to the lentils and mix well. Fold
in the mint and season with salt and pepper. Serve at room
temperature.

Serves 6

Asparagus and Potatoes with Almonds and Mint

24 small red new potatoes, about 3 lb
   (1.5 kg) total weight
6 tablespoons (3 fl oz/90 ml) olive oil
salt and ground pepper to taste
2 lb (1 kg) fresh asparagus
ice water as needed
1 cup (8 fl oz/250 ml) Chicken Stock
   (*page 10*) or broth
2 cloves garlic, minced
½ cup (2 oz/60 g) toasted sliced (flaked)
   or slivered blanched almonds
   (*see glossary, page 107*)
½ cup (¾ oz/20 g) chopped fresh mint
   or basil

In this quickly assembled vegetable combination, you can instead put pine nuts with the mint or basil with the almonds. The asparagus can be cooked up to 4 hours before serving.

Preheat an oven to 400°F (200°C).

Place the potatoes in a baking pan, coat them with about 2 tablespoons of the olive oil, and sprinkle with salt and pepper. Roast until the potatoes are cooked through but firm, 25–35 minutes depending upon their size. Remove from the oven and let stand until cool enough to handle.

Meanwhile, prepare the asparagus: Snap off the tough end of each stalk. If the stalks are thick, using a vegetable peeler and starting about 2 inches (5 cm) below the tip, peel off the thin outer skin. In a frying pan, pour in water to a depth of 2 inches (5 cm), salt lightly, and bring to a boil. Lay the asparagus in the pan and cook until tender-crisp, 3–5 minutes; the timing will depend upon the thickness. Drain the asparagus and plunge them into ice water to halt the cooking, then drain and pat dry. Cut the asparagus into 2-inch (5-cm) lengths.

Cut the cooled potatoes into quarters. In a very large frying pan over medium heat, warm the remaining 4 tablespoons (2 fl oz/60 ml) olive oil. Add the potatoes and heat through, turning occasionally. Add the asparagus, stock or broth, and garlic and simmer for a few minutes to heat through. Season with salt and pepper, then add the almonds and mint or basil. Transfer to a warmed serving bowl and serve immediately.

Serves 6

Potato and Sage Gratin

3 cups (24 fl oz/750 ml) heavy (double) cream, or more if needed

4 cloves garlic, sliced

8–10 fresh sage leaves, chopped, plus whole leaves for garnish

1½ teaspoons salt

1 teaspoon ground pepper

¼ teaspoon ground nutmeg

6 large white boiling potatoes, peeled and sliced ¼ inch (6 mm) thick

Fresh sage leaves and a hint of nutmeg perfume these sliced and baked potatoes, a hearty accompaniment for roast beef or any other meat or poultry main course. This dish can be assembled up to 2 hours before baking and serving.

Preheat an oven to 375°F (190°C). Generously butter a 3-qt (3-l) baking dish.

In a saucepan over medium-high heat, combine the cream, garlic, and chopped sage. Reduce the heat to low and simmer for 15 minutes to blend the flavors. Season with the salt, pepper, and nutmeg and remove from the heat.

Arrange the potatoes in overlapping rows in the baking dish. Pour the sage cream evenly over them. The cream should just cover the potatoes; add a bit more if needed to cover. Cover with aluminum foil.

Bake for 30 minutes. Remove the foil and continue to bake until the potatoes are tender but still hold their shape, about 20 minutes longer. Remove from the oven, garnish with a few whole sage leaves, and serve immediately.

Serves 6

Chanterelles, Chestnuts, and Pearl Onions with Thyme

1 lb (500 g) chestnuts
2 cups (16 fl oz/500 ml) water
1 lb (500 g) pearl onions or cipolline
2 lb (1 kg) chanterelles or cremini
   mushrooms, brushed clean
½ cup (4 oz/125 g) unsalted butter
2 tablespoons chopped fresh thyme
½ cup (4 fl oz/125 ml) Chicken Stock
   (*page 10*) or broth, or as needed
salt and ground pepper to taste

Here is a sumptuous side dish to accompany holiday roast poultry. Peeling fresh chestnuts is a painstaking task, as they must be hot for the inner skin to come off. You can use purchased canned peeled chestnuts instead.

⊕

*U*sing a small, sharp knife, cut a cross in the rounded side of each chestnut. In a small saucepan over high heat, bring the water to a boil. Add the chestnuts. Reduce the heat to low, cover, and simmer until the chestnuts are tender, about 30 minutes. Drain the chestnuts and while they are still hot, remove both the hard outer shell and the furry inner brown skin.

Using a small, sharp, knife, carefully trim away the roots from the onions without cutting into the ends. Cut a shallow cross into the stem end of each onion to prevent it from telescoping while cooking. In a saucepan over high heat, combine the onions with water to cover and bring to a boil. Reduce the heat to medium and simmer, uncovered, until barely tender, 8–10 minutes. Drain, let cool slightly, and then slip off the peels. Set aside.

Preheat an oven to 350°F (180°C).

If the mushrooms are small, leave them whole; if they are large, slice them thickly. In a large sauté pan over high heat, melt half of the butter. Add half of the mushrooms and sauté until softened, 3–5 minutes. Transfer to a bowl. Repeat with the remaining butter and mushrooms and add to the bowl.

Combine the cooked chestnuts, onions, mushrooms, and the thyme. Add enough stock or broth to moisten the mixture and season with salt and pepper. Transfer to a baking dish. Bake until heated through, about 15 minutes. Serve at once.

Serves 12

Jasmine Rice with Shredded Zucchini

1 lb (500 g) small zucchini (courgettes)
salt for sprinkling, plus ½ teaspoon
½ cup (4 fl oz/125 ml) coconut milk
1¼ cups (10 fl oz/310 ml) water
1 teaspoon peeled and grated fresh ginger
1 cup (7 oz/220 g) jasmine rice, rinsed
   and drained
3 tablespoons unsalted butter
1 tablespoon minced green (spring)
   onion, including some tender
   green tops
ground nutmeg to taste
grated zest and juice of 1 lemon

Jasmine rice, a long-grain white rice grown in Thailand, has a fragrant and slightly nutty aroma and flavor. Paired here with mild zucchini, coconut milk, and fresh ginger, it makes a delightful accompaniment to roast lamb and chicken.

Trim the zucchini and shred on the medium holes of a handheld shredder. In a colander set over a bowl, layer half of the zucchini. Sprinkle with salt, then top with the remaining zucchini and again sprinkle with salt. Set aside for 25–30 minutes to drain off the bitter juice. Then, pick up the zucchini by small handfuls and squeeze out the released juice. Return the zucchini to the colander, rinse with cold running water to wash out the salt, and again squeeze out the moisture; set aside.

In a heavy saucepan, stir together the coconut milk, water, ginger, and ½ teaspoon salt. Bring to a rapid boil and gradually add the rice. Reduce the heat to very low, cover, and cook until just tender and the liquid has been absorbed, 15–20 minutes. Remove from the heat and let stand, covered, for 5 minutes. Uncover and carefully fluff the rice with a fork. Cover to keep warm until serving.

In a frying pan over medium-high heat, melt the butter. Add the zucchini, green onion, and a little nutmeg, and cook, stirring and tossing, until tender but still opaque, 4–5 minutes, adding about 1 teaspoon or so of the lemon juice toward the end of cooking. Taste and adjust the seasonings with more lemon juice and/or salt.

Arrange the rice around the edge of a warmed serving plate, forming a ring. Spoon the zucchini mixture into the center and sprinkle with the lemon zest. Serve at once.

Serves 4

Glazed Carrots and Parsnips

1½ lb (750 g) carrots

1 lb (500 g) parsnips

1 cup (8 fl oz/250 ml) water

½ teaspoon salt

4 tablespoons (2 oz/60 g) unsalted butter

½ cup (3½ oz/105 g) firmly packed
  brown sugar

3 tablespoons Madeira wine

½ teaspoon peeled and finely grated fresh
  ginger

fresh mint, parsley, or sage, chopped or
  whole sprigs

These two root vegetables complement each other nicely. They can be prepared in advance up to the point of glazing. Additional carrots may be substituted for the parsnips.

⊕

Peel the carrots and parsnips. Cut into 3-inch (7.5-cm) lengths. Cut each piece lengthwise in half, then cut the thick upper portions lengthwise into quarters so the pieces are of equal size for cooking. In a small saucepan over medium heat, combine the carrots, parsnips, water, salt, and 2 tablespoons of the butter. Bring to a simmer, cover tightly, reduce the heat to low, and simmer very gently until just tender, 10–15 minutes. Drain and set aside.

In a frying pan over medium heat, melt the remaining 2 tablespoons butter. Add the brown sugar, wine, and ginger, and cook, stirring constantly, until the sugar dissolves. Reduce the heat to low and continue to cook until the mixture is reduced and thickened, 2–3 minutes. Add the carrots and parsnips and toss until well coated. Cook until the vegetables are heated through, 2–3 minutes.

Transfer to a warmed serving dish and garnish with mint, parsley, or sage. Serve immediately.

Serves 8–10

Seafood Stew

2 fennel bulbs, 1½–2 lb (750 g–1 kg)
 total weight

3 tablespoons extra-virgin olive oil, plus
 extra for brushing on bread

3 cloves garlic, chopped

1 lb (500 g) ripe plum (Roma) tomatoes,
 peeled, seeded, and chopped
 (*see glossary, page 107*)

2 bay leaves

4 cups (32 fl oz/1 l) water

2 cups (16 fl oz/500 ml) bottled clam
 juice

1 cup (8 fl oz/250 ml) dry white wine

1 tablespoon lemon juice

2 teaspoons salt

pinch of red pepper flakes

12–14 mussels in the shell, well scrubbed
 and debearded

2 lb (1 kg) assorted white fish fillets such
 as sea bass, halibut, red snapper, and
 sole, in any combination, cut into
 2-inch (5-cm) pieces

½ lb (250 g) small shrimp (prawns),
 peeled, with the tail fin intact, and
 deveined (*see glossary, page 107*)

4 slices coarse country bread, each about
 ½ inch (12 mm) thick

coarsely chopped fresh flat-leaf (Italian)
 parsley

Good country-style Italian or French bread is an absolute necessity for use in making this delightful Mediterranean main course.

❋

Cut off the stems and feathery tops and any bruised outer stalks from the fennel bulbs; reserve any attractive tops for garnish, if you like. Cut the bulbs in half lengthwise, and then cut each half lengthwise into 4 wedges; set aside.

Preheat an oven to 325°F (165°C).

In a large saucepan over medium-low heat, warm the 3 table-spoons olive oil. Add the garlic and sauté until it begins to change color, 1–2 minutes. Add the tomatoes, fennel, and bay leaves and cook, uncovered, until the tomatoes start to release their juices, 8–10 minutes. Stir in the water, clam juice, wine, lemon juice, salt, and red pepper flakes. Cover partially, reduce the heat to low, and cook until the fennel is almost tender, 20–25 minutes.

Meanwhile, discard any mussels that do not close to the touch; set aside. When the fennel is almost tender, add the fish pieces, cover, and barely simmer over low heat for 10 minutes. Add the mussels and shrimp and continue to simmer until the fish is opaque throughout when pierced with a sharp knife, the shrimp are pink, and the mussels are open, another 5–6 minutes. Discard any mussels that did not open. Taste and adjust the seasonings.

Brush each bread slice with oil and arrange on a baking sheet, oiled side up. Warm in the oven for a few minutes.

To serve, place a warm bread slice in each of 4 deep, warmed soup bowls. Ladle the stew over the bread and garnish with parsley. Serve at once.

Serves 4

Citrus-Marinated Cornish Hens

4 Cornish hens, 1½ lb (750 g) each
2 teaspoons finely grated lemon zest
½ cup (4 fl oz/125 ml) lemon or lime juice
½ cup (4 fl oz/125 ml) orange juice
2 cloves garlic, minced
2 tablespoons minced shallots or green (spring) onions
½ teaspoon salt
½ jalapeño chile, seeded and minced
10 fresh thyme or rosemary sprigs, plus sprigs for garnish
lemon, lime, and/or orange slices

This dish is well suited for a festive lunch or dinner. Get a head start on your preparations and marinate the hens at least 2 hours before cooking or as long as overnight.

✳

*B*utterfly the hens: Place each hen, breast side down, on a cutting board. Insert a sharp knife through the neck cavity of each bird and carefully cut down one side of the backbone. (Or use heavy-duty kitchen scissors.) Then cut along the other side of the backbone, lift it up, and remove it. Turn the hen breast side up. Using the heel of your hand, press down firmly on the breastbone to flatten it. Place in a shallow dish in a single layer.

In a small bowl, stir together the lemon zest, lemon or lime juice, orange juice, garlic, shallots or green onions, salt, and jalapeño chile. Pour evenly over the hens and turn to coat. Cover and refrigerate for at least 2 hours or for up to overnight.

Preheat an oven to 425°F (220°C). Brush a large roasting pan with vegetable oil.

Remove the hens from the marinade and pat them dry with paper towels. Reserve the marinade. Place 5 of the thyme or rosemary sprigs in the prepared pan and put the hens, skin side up, on top in a single layer, laying them flat. Tuck the remaining 5 herb sprigs around the hens.

Roast for 15 minutes. Brush with some of the reserved marinade, then reduce the heat to 325°F (165°C). Roast for 15 minutes and brush again with the reserved marinade. Continue roasting until the skin is well browned and the meat is no longer pink when cut at the bone, about 15 minutes longer.

Transfer the hens to a warmed platter or individual plates and spoon the pan juices over the top. Garnish with herb sprigs and lemon, lime, and/or orange slices. Serve at once.

Serves 4

Baked Chicken and Sweet Potatoes

1 chicken, 3½–4 lb (1.75–2 kg), cut into serving pieces

3 tablespoons unsalted butter

2 tablespoons vegetable oil

2 or 3 sweet potatoes, 1½–2 lb (750 g–1 kg) total weight, peeled and cut crosswise into slices ½ inch (12 mm) thick

8–10 shallots, thinly sliced

½ cup (4 fl oz/125 ml) pure apple juice or calvados, plus extra juice if needed

½ cup (4 fl oz/125 ml) Chicken Stock (*page 10*) or broth, plus extra stock or broth if needed

6–8 fresh sage leaves, plus 2 or 3 sprigs for garnish

salt and ground pepper to taste

1 tablespoon all-purpose (plain) flour

¼ cup (2 fl oz/60 ml) heavy (double) cream

Preheat an oven to 375°F (190°C). Butter a baking dish large enough to hold the chicken and potatoes in a single layer.

Cut the 2 chicken breast halves in half crosswise. Cut the thighs and legs apart. Remove the wing tips and save along with the back for another use. You should have 10 pieces. Remove any fat from them. Rinse and pat dry with paper towels.

In a sauté pan over medium-high heat, melt 2 tablespoons of the butter with the oil. Add half of the chicken and quickly sear until golden, 4–5 minutes on each side. Transfer to the prepared dish. Repeat with the remaining chicken. Arrange the potato slices among the chicken pieces in the baking dish.

Reduce the heat to medium-low and add the shallots to the pan. Sauté until translucent, 2–3 minutes. Add half each of the apple juice or calvados and stock or broth and deglaze the pan. Bring to a boil and pour over the chicken and potatoes. Tuck the sage leaves around the chicken. Sprinkle with salt and pepper.

Bake until the potatoes are tender and the chicken is opaque throughout, 45–50 minutes. Using a slotted spoon, transfer the chicken and potatoes to a warmed serving dish and cover to keep warm. Skim off the fat from the juices and pour into a pitcher.

In a small saucepan over medium-low heat, melt the remaining 1 tablespoon butter. Add the flour and cook, stirring, until bubbly, 1–2 minutes. Raise the heat to medium. Stirring constantly, gradually add the remaining ¼ cup (2 fl oz/60 ml) each apple juice or calvados and stock or broth and the pan juices. Stir until the mixture thickens and comes to a boil, 3–4 minutes. Add the cream and cook for a few seconds. Thin, if desired, with apple juice or broth; taste and adjust the seasonings.

Pour the sauce over the chicken and potatoes. Garnish with sage sprigs and serve.

Serves 4

Grilled Shrimp with Charmoula

24–32 large shrimp (prawns), peeled, with the tail fin intact, and deveined (*see glossary, page 107*)

¼ cup (2 fl oz/60 ml) lemon juice

2 teaspoons paprika

¼ teaspoon cayenne pepper

1 teaspoon ground cumin

3 cloves garlic, minced

¼ cup (⅓ oz/10 g) chopped fresh flat-leaf (Italian) parsley

¼ cup (⅓ oz/10 g) chopped fresh cilantro (fresh coriander)

½ cup (4 fl oz/125 ml) extra-virgin olive oil

salt and ground black pepper to taste

FOR THE COUSCOUS:

3 cups (24 fl oz/750 ml) water

¼ cup (2 oz/60 g) unsalted butter

1 teaspoon ground cinnamon

1 teaspoon salt

2 cups (12 oz/375 g) instant couscous

Charmoula is an intensely flavored Moroccan marinade and sauce used on fish and shellfish. Here it flavors shrimp—an easy main course for an al fresco lunch or dinner.

❈

Slip the shrimp onto 8 bamboo or metal skewers: For each serving, hold 2 skewers parallel and thread 6–8 shrimp onto them so that 1 skewer passes through near the tail of each shrimp and the other skewer passes through near the head. Place in a baking pan large enough to hold the skewers flat.

In a bowl, whisk together the lemon juice, paprika, cayenne, cumin, garlic, parsley, cilantro, olive oil, salt, and black pepper. Pour half of the mixture over the shrimp and turn the skewers to coat evenly. Cover and refrigerate for 2–4 hours. Reserve the remaining marinade to use for a sauce.

Prepare a fire in a charcoal grill or preheat a broiler (griller).

Meanwhile, make the couscous: In a saucepan, combine the water, butter, cinnamon, and salt and bring to a boil. Spread the couscous evenly in a shallow, 9-inch (23-cm) square baking pan. Pour the hot water mixture over the couscous. Stir well, then cover and allow the couscous to absorb the liquid, about 10 minutes.

Remove the skewers from the marinade and discard the marinade. Arrange on the grill rack 4–6 inches (10–15 cm) from the fire, or place on the broiler pan and slip under the broiler about the same distance from the heat source. Grill or broil, turning once, until pink, 3–4 minutes on each side.

Uncover the couscous and fluff with a fork. Spoon onto individual plates. Remove the shrimp from the skewers and arrange on the couscous. Spoon on the reserved sauce and serve.

Serves 4

Poussins Glazed with Mustard and Maple Syrup

6 poussins, about 1 lb (500 g) each
2 teaspoons dry mustard
½ teaspoon ground cinnamon
2 tablespoons cider vinegar
⅔ cup (5 fl oz/160 ml) pure maple syrup
3 tablespoons Dijon mustard
2 tablespoons soy sauce
salt and ground pepper to taste
olive oil for brushing

Take care not to overcook these small chickens; when done, their flesh remains slightly pink. For an extra special occasion, substitute quail for the poussins—allowing 2 for each serving.

Butterfly the poussins: Place each poussin, breast side down, on a cutting board. Insert a sharp knife through the neck cavity of each bird and carefully cut down one side of the backbone. (Or use heavy-duty kitchen scissors.) Then cut along the other side of the backbone, lift it up, and remove it. Turn the bird breast side up. Using the heel of your hand, press down firmly on the breastbone to flatten it. Place in a shallow dish in a single layer.

In a small bowl, stir together the dry mustard, cinnamon, and vinegar to form a paste. Add the maple syrup, Dijon mustard, and soy sauce and mix well. Spread half of this mixture evenly over the birds and turn to coat. Cover and refrigerate for at least 2 hours or for up to 8 hours. Reserve the remaining paste for basting.

Prepare a fire in a charcoal grill. Oil the grill rack and position it 4–6 inches (10–15 cm) above the fire. Alternatively, preheat a broiler (griller). Sprinkle the birds with salt and pepper and brush with a little olive oil. Place over medium-hot coals, flesh side down, or place on a broiler pan and slip under the broiler about 4 inches (10 cm) from the heat source. Grill or broil until nicely browned, about 5 minutes. Brush with the remaining paste, turn, and cook until nicely browned on the second side, 5 minutes longer.

Remove from the grill or broiler and transfer to warmed individual plates. Serve hot.

Serves 6

Chicken with Oranges and Watercress

¼ cup (2 oz/60 g) unsalted butter
4 whole chicken legs with thigh attached
½ lemon
salt to taste
zest of ½ orange, cut into thin strips
2 navel or large Valencia oranges, peeled and cut into segments (*see glossary, page 105*)
1 large bunch watercress, tough stems removed

This dish is a special treat for fans of dark-meat poultry. Cutting off the knobby drumstick joint severs the tough tendon, making the meat easy to cut off the bone once cooked. Be sure to strip away the orange zest before you peel and segment the oranges.

❋

Preheat a broiler (griller). Line a broiler pan with aluminum foil.

In a small saucepan over low heat, melt the butter. Remove from the heat and set aside. Rinse the chicken legs and pat dry with paper towels. Using a meat cleaver or a large chef's knife, chop the end joint off the drumsticks. Rub the legs with the cut lemon and brush generously with some of the melted butter. Sprinkle lightly with salt.

Arrange the chicken legs, skin side down, on the prepared pan. Slip under the broiler 5–6 inches (13–15 cm) from the heat source and broil (grill) for 10–12 minutes. Turn skin side up and continue to broil, brushing often with the remaining butter, until the skin is crisp and golden and juices run clear when the thickest part of the thigh is pierced, about 10 minutes longer.

Bring a small saucepan three-fourths full of water to a boil and add the zest strips. Boil for 2 minutes, then drain and set aside.

When the chicken legs are done, transfer to a warmed platter. Garnish with the orange zest slivers, orange segments, and watercress. Serve immediately.

Serves 4

Poached Salmon

3 qt (3 l) water, or as needed
3 cups (24 fl oz/750 ml) dry white wine
3 yellow onions, sliced
3 carrots, peeled and sliced
6 fresh thyme sprigs
3 celery stalks, sliced
1 large bunch fresh parsley
3 tablespoons sea salt
¼ teaspoon peppercorns
3 bay leaves
1 whole salmon, 6 lb (3 kg), scaled and cleaned
1 lemon, sliced
½ cucumber, sliced paper-thin

A whole fish makes a spectacular hot or cold main course for a dinner party or an elegant buffet. Offer a hollandaise sauce or a green mayonnaise flavored with finely chopped fresh parsley or tarragon.

Select a fish poacher or roasting pan in which the salmon will fit comfortably. (If the fish is too long for the pan, cut off the head—or ask your fishmonger to do it.) Add the water, wine, onions, carrots, thyme, celery, half of the parsley sprigs, the sea salt, peppercorns, and bay leaves to the pan and place over medium-high heat. Bring just to a boil, reduce the heat to medium, and simmer, uncovered, for 20–30 minutes to make a full-flavored bouillon. Reduce the heat so the liquid simmers very gently.

Measure the fish at its thickest point, then determine the poaching time by allowing 10 minutes for each 1 inch (2.5 cm) of thickness. Cut a piece of cheesecloth (muslin) about 24 inches (60 cm) long. Lay the fish in the middle of the cheesecloth and, holding the two ends, carefully lower the salmon into the simmering bouillon; lay the cheesecloth ends on top. If the bouillon does not cover the fish, add hot water as needed.

Cover and gently simmer for the determined time. To test for doneness, insert a knife into the thickest part; the flesh at the center should be opaque. Turn off the heat and let the fish rest in the liquid for about 5 minutes.

With the aid of the cheesecloth, carefully lift out the fish and place on a warmed platter, slipping the cheesecloth free. Carefully peel off the skin from the top side of the salmon and discard. Gently turn the salmon over and peel off the skin from the opposite side. Using a thin knife, loosen the flesh from the bone to make it easier to serve. Garnish with the lemon and cucumber slices and the remaining parsley sprigs.

Serves 8

Roast Chicken with Herbs

FOR THE CHICKEN:

1 large roasting chicken, about 6 lb (3 kg)

1 lemon, halved

salt and ground pepper to taste

paprika (optional)

FOR THE BASTE:

½ cup (4 fl oz/125 ml) olive oil

¼ cup (2 fl oz/60 ml) lemon juice

3 cloves garlic, smashed

1 tablespoon chopped fresh sage

1 teaspoon chopped fresh thyme

1 teaspoon ground pepper

Fresh lemon juice, garlic, and lots of fresh herbs give this classic roast chicken a sprightly flavor.

Preheat an oven to 375°F (190°C).

Rinse the bird inside and out, pat dry with paper towels, and then rub inside and out with the cut lemon. Rub the cavity lightly with a little salt and pepper. Place the chicken, breast side down, on a rack in a roasting pan. Sprinkle with salt, pepper, and a little paprika, if desired.

To make the baste, in a small bowl, stir together the olive oil, lemon juice, garlic, sage, thyme, and pepper.

Roast the chicken for 45 minutes, brushing or spooning the baste over the bird every 15 minutes.

Turn the chicken breast side up and continue to roast, basting every 15 minutes, until tender and the juices run clear when a thigh is pierced with a skewer or long fork, about 30 minutes longer. To test with an instant-read thermometer, insert it into the thickest part of the thigh away from the bone; it should register 180°F (82°C).

Remove from the oven, transfer to a cutting board, tent loosely with aluminum foil, and let rest for about 15 minutes.

Carve the chicken, arrange on a warm platter, and serve immediately.

Serves 4

Roast Pork Loin and Onions

1½ lb (750 g) small boiling onions, about
    1 inch (2.5 cm) in diameter (about 30)
1 center-cut boneless pork loin, 2½–3 lb
    (1.25–1.5 kg), trimmed of most fat and
    tied in several places
1–2 tablespoons olive oil
2 teaspoons chopped fresh thyme, plus
    6 sprigs
salt and ground pepper to taste
½ cup (4 fl oz/125 ml) dry white wine,
    plus extra wine for basting
1 teaspoon cornstarch (cornflour) mixed
    with 1 tablespoon water

Position a rack in the lower third of an oven and preheat to 425°F (220°C). Lightly coat a heavy roasting pan with olive oil.

Trim the onions, then peel and cut a shallow cross in the stem end. Fill a saucepan three-fourths full with water and bring to a boil. Add the onions, return the water to a boil, and boil for 2 minutes. Drain and set aside.

Wipe any moisture from the pork loin with paper towels, then rub all over with the olive oil. Sprinkle with the chopped thyme and season lightly with salt and pepper. Place the pork loin, fat side up, in the roasting pan (without a rack) and add the ½ cup (4 fl oz/ 125 ml) wine. Surround the meat with the onions.

Roast, stirring the onions occasionally and basting the meat and onions a few times with the extra wine or the pan juices, until the loin and onions are lightly golden and the juices run clear when the loin is pierced with a knife, 50–70 minutes. To test for doneness, insert an instant-read thermometer into the center of the meat; it should read 160°–165°F (71°–74°C).

Remove from the oven and transfer the roast to a warmed platter; cover loosely with aluminum foil and set aside in a warm place. Using a slotted spoon, transfer the onions to a bowl and cover to keep warm. Pour the juices from the pan into a medium saucepan. Let stand for a few minutes to allow the fat to rise to the surface, then skim off the fat with a large spoon and discard. Stir the cornstarch mixture into the juices, place over medium-low heat, and bring to a boil, stirring constantly. When the mixture thickens, season to taste with salt and pepper. If it thickens too much, add a little water or wine to thin to the proper consistency. Return the onions to the sauce and turn to coat well.

To serve, cut the meat into slices ½ inch (12 mm) thick and arrange on the platter. Surround the meat with the onions and their sauce. Garnish with the thyme sprigs.

Serves 6

Rack of Spring Lamb with Mediterranean Flavors

Try this main course for any springtime celebration. The marinade combines Greek, Turkish, and North African flavors.

✳

To make the marinade, in a food processor or blender, combine the onion, garlic, lemon juice, lemon zest, orange zest, mustard, cumin, allspice, cayenne, thyme, and black pepper. Pulse or blend to a purée. Add the olive oil until the mixture is blended.

Place the lamb in a nonaluminum container, add the marinade, and turn to coat evenly. Cover and refrigerate for at least 6 hours or for up to 2 days.

To cook the racks, preheat an oven to 350°F (180°C).

In a cast-iron frying pan over high heat or on a hot griddle, sear the racks until browned on all sides, 6–8 minutes. Transfer to a roasting pan.

Roast in the oven until an instant-read thermometer inserted in the center of a rack reads 125°F (52°C), 10–12 minutes. Remove from the oven and transfer to a cutting board. Tent loosely with aluminum foil and let rest for 10 minutes. The meat will be medium-rare. Slice the lamb between the ribs, divide the ribs evenly among warmed individual plates, and serve.

To cook the chops, prepare a fire in a charcoal grill. Oil the grill rack and position it 4–6 inches (10–15 cm) above the fire. Alternatively, preheat a broiler (griller). Brush the chops with olive oil, sprinkle with salt, and place on the grill rack or slip under the broiler about 4 inches (10 cm) from the heat source. Grill or broil, turning once, 3 minutes on each side for rare or 4 minutes on each side for medium-rare. Arrange 2 lamb chops on each warmed plate to serve.

Serves 6

FOR THE MARINADE:
1 yellow onion, grated
2 tablespoons minced garlic
3 tablespoons lemon juice
grated zest of 1 lemon
grated zest of 1 orange
1 tablespoon Dijon mustard
2 teaspoons ground cumin
1 teaspoon ground allspice
½ teaspoon cayenne pepper
2 tablespoons chopped fresh thyme or
  2 teaspoons dried thyme
1 teaspoon ground black pepper
½ cup (4 fl oz/125 ml) olive oil

FOR THE LAMB:
2 racks of lamb, trimmed, or 12 lamb
  chops
olive oil for brushing
salt to taste

Fillet of Beef with Paprika, Coriander, and Cumin

1 beef fillet, about 3½ lb (1.75 kg)
3 tablespoons paprika
2 tablespoons ground black pepper
1 tablespoon ground coriander
2 teaspoons ground cumin
1 teaspoon ground nutmeg
¼ teaspoon cayenne pepper
1 tablespoon salt
hot-sweet mustard

The beef, which takes on an aromatic flavor from the spice rub, requires 4 days of marinating. You can serve it rare, leaving the end slices for those who like their meat well done. The recipe doubles easily for a gala buffet.

✳

*T*rim the fillet of any visible fat and silver skin. In a small bowl, stir together the paprika, black pepper, coriander, cumin, nutmeg, and cayenne. Spread the spice mixture evenly over the beef. Place the meat in a large nonaluminum container, cover, and refrigerate for 4 days. On the third day, sprinkle the meat with the salt.

Remove the meat from the refrigerator and bring to room temperature, about 1 hour.

Preheat an oven to 350°F (180°C).

Place a stove-top griddle or a large cast-iron frying pan over high heat and heat until very hot. Place the fillet on the griddle or in the pan and sear, turning as needed, until well browned on all sides, 6–8 minutes total. Transfer the meat to a roasting pan. Roast 10–15 minutes per pound (500 g) or until an instant-read thermometer inserted in the center of the fillet registers 120°F (49°C) for rare, or until done to your liking. Remove from the oven and transfer to a cutting board. Tent loosely with aluminum foil and let rest for 15 minutes. Slice thinly and arrange on a warmed platter. Serve with the hot-sweet mustard.

Serves 6

Peaches in Wine

6 ripe peaches

2 cups (16 fl oz/500 ml) fruity white
  wine such as Asti Spumante, moscato,
  or Riesling; or a light, fruity red wine
  such as Lambrusco or Beaujolais

½ cup (4 oz/125 g) sugar

You might be hard pressed to decide which is more pleasurable—the wine-scented peaches or the peach-flavored wine. Making this summertime dessert could not be simpler. Nectarines also work well.

✿

*B*ring a pot of water to a boil. Drop in 1 peach at a time and leave for 5 seconds. Using a slotted spoon, transfer to a work surface and let cool briefly, then peel. Cut the peaches in half and discard the pits.

   In an attractive glass bowl, combine the wine and sugar. Stir until the sugar dissolves. Place the peach halves in the wine. Chill for 1 hour, then serve.

Serves 6

Warm Blueberry Shortcakes

FOR THE SHORTCAKES:

1¾ cups (9 oz/280 g) all-purpose (plain) flour

½ teaspoon salt

1 tablespoon baking powder

2 teaspoons sugar

6 tablespoons (3 oz/90 g) chilled unsalted butter, cut into bits

1 cup (8 fl oz/250 ml) milk or heavy (double) cream

grated zest of 1 orange or 2 lemons

about 3 tablespoons unsalted butter, melted, or heavy (double) cream

FOR THE BLUEBERRY COMPOTE:

6 cups (1½ lb/750 g) fresh or thawed frozen blueberries

2 tablespoons lemon juice

1 teaspoon ground cinnamon

1½ cups (12 oz/375 g) sugar

grated zest of 1 orange or 1 lemon

FOR THE MAPLE WHIPPED CREAM:

1 cup (8 fl oz/250 ml) heavy (double) cream

2 tablespoons pure maple syrup

¼ teaspoon vanilla extract (essence)

*P*reheat an oven to 450°F (230°C).

To make the shortcakes, in a bowl, stir together the flour, salt, baking powder, and sugar. Add the chilled butter to the flour mixture and using a pastry blender or 2 knives, cut it in until the mixture resembles cornmeal. Make a well in the center and add the 1 cup (8 fl oz/250 ml) milk or cream and the citrus zest. Stir vigorously until the dough comes free from the sides of the bowl, about 1 minute. Turn out the dough onto a lightly floured board and knead gently and quickly for about 12 turns, or until the dough is no longer sticky. Pat into a round about ½ inch (12 mm) thick.

Using a round biscuit cutter 2¼ inches (5.5 cm) in diameter and dipping it into flour each time, cut out 12 biscuits. Place on an ungreased baking sheet and brush the tops with the melted butter or the cream. Bake until pale gold, 12–15 minutes.

Meanwhile, make the compote: In a heavy saucepan over medium heat, combine 4 cups (1 lb/500 g) of the blueberries with the lemon juice, cinnamon, sugar, and citrus zest. Bring to a simmer, stirring occasionally, and cook until thickened and hot, about 5 minutes. Stir in the remaining blueberries, remove from the heat, and set aside.

To make the whipped cream, in a bowl, combine the cream, maple syrup, and vanilla. Using an electric mixer or a whisk, beat until soft peaks form.

When the shortcakes are ready, remove from the oven, let cool slightly, then split the warm biscuits in half horizontally. Place 2 bottoms on each of 6 individual plates. Spoon half of the blueberry compote on the biscuit bottoms, add a dollop of the whipped cream, and then add a little more compote to each. Top with the remaining biscuit halves. Spoon on the remaining compote and serve at once.

Serves 6

Blue Plum Tart

Basic Pie Pastry (*page 13*)

½ cup (2½ oz/75 g) plus 2 tablespoons hazelnuts (filberts), toasted and skinned (*see glossary, page 107*)

½ cup (4 oz/125 g) plus 2 tablespoons sugar

½ teaspoon ground cinnamon

½ teaspoon ground ginger

3 tablespoons unsalted butter, at room temperature

16–20 Italian prune plums, halved and pitted

¾ cup (7½ oz/235 g) orange marmalade

whipped cream flavored with orange zest (optional)

*P*reheat an oven to 400°F (200°C). On a lightly floured work surface, roll out the pastry into a 10-by-13-inch (25-by-33-cm) rectangle or a 12-inch (30-cm) round. Drape the rectangle or round over the rolling pin and carefully transfer it to an 8-by-11-inch (20-by-28-cm) rectangular tart pan or a 10-inch (25-cm) round tart pan with removable bottom. Gently ease the pastry into the pan and trim the edges even with the pan rim. Place in the freezer for 30 minutes.

Meanwhile, finely chop the ½ cup (2½ oz/75 g) hazelnuts and coarsely chop the remaining 2 tablespoons hazelnuts. In a food processor or bowl, combine the finely chopped hazelnuts, the ½ cup (4 oz/ 125 g) sugar, the cinnamon, ginger, and butter. Pulse or cut in the butter with a pastry blender or 2 knives until blended into a paste. Transfer to the pastry-lined tart pan and press into an even layer. Top with the plums, arranging them cut side down in overlapping rows. Sprinkle with the remaining 2 tablespoons sugar.

Bake for 10 minutes. Reduce the oven temperature to 350°F (180°C) and continue to bake until the plums are bubbly and the crust is golden, 20–30 minutes longer.

Meanwhile, in a small saucepan over low heat, melt the orange marmalade. Strain through a sieve into a bowl and keep warm.

When the tart is done, remove from the oven, place on a rack, and brush the melted marmalade over the plums. Sprinkle with the 2 tablespoons coarsely chopped hazelnuts and let cool. Carefully remove the pan sides and slide the tart off the pan bottom onto a serving plate.

Serve at room temperature. Accompany each piece with a dollop of orange-flavored whipped cream, if desired.

Serves 8

Chocolate Pots de Crème with Candied Rose Petals

FOR THE POTS DE CRÈME:

1⅓ cups (10 fl oz/310 ml) heavy (double) cream

4 oz (125 g) semisweet (plain) chocolate, grated

1 tablespoon plus 1 teaspoon firmly packed light brown sugar

pinch of salt

4 egg yolks

1 teaspoon vanilla extract (essence)

FOR THE CANDIED ROSE PETALS:

rose petals

1 egg white, lightly beaten

½ cup (3½ oz/105 g) superfine (caster) sugar

Rich, creamy, and intensely chocolaty, these are among the most elegant of desserts. You can find candied rose petals in gourmet shops, but making your own is easy. Be sure to use only roses that are pesticide free.

❃

To make the pots de crème, place the cream, chocolate, brown sugar, and salt in the top pan of a double boiler or in a heatproof bowl. Place over (not touching) simmering water in the lower pan and heat until small bubbles appear along the edges of the pan or bowl. In a small bowl, whisk the egg yolks until blended, then whisk in a few tablespoons of the hot chocolate cream to warm them. Gradually stir the yolk mixture back into the chocolate cream and cook over simmering water, stirring, until thickened, about 10 minutes.

Remove from the heat, stir in the vanilla, and pour into pot de crème cups or small custard cups. Let cool uncovered, then cover and refrigerate until cold, about 2 hours or for up to overnight. Remove from the refrigerator about 30 minutes before serving.

Meanwhile, make the candied rose petals: Working with 1 petal at a time, hold the petal with tweezers and gently brush with the egg white. Then sprinkle both sides with the superfine sugar, coating evenly. As each petal is coated, place it on a wire rack to dry completely.

To serve, garnish the pots de crème with the rose petals and serve at room temperature.

Serves 4

Mandarin Orange Custard Tart

FOR THE TART:

6 egg yolks

½ cup (4 fl oz/125 ml) mandarin orange
  juice

¼ cup (2 fl oz/60 ml) lemon juice

¾ cup (6 oz/185 g) granulated sugar

¼ cup (2 oz/60 g) unsalted butter, cut
  into bits

grated zest of 3 mandarin oranges

1 tablespoon mandarin orange liqueur

Basic Pie Pastry (*page 13*)

FOR THE TOPPING:

1 cup (8 fl oz/250 ml) heavy (double)
  cream

2 tablespoons sifted confectioners' (icing)
  sugar

grated zest of 2 mandarin oranges

mandarin orange liqueur to taste

Sweet-tart mandarin oranges make an elegant curdlike filling for a festive dessert. Be sure to grate the mandarin zest for the topping before you juice the fruit for the filling.

❁

*T*o make the filling, whisk together the egg yolks, mandarin orange and lemon juices, and granulated sugar until well blended. Strain into the top pan of a double boiler or a heatproof bowl and place over (not touching) simmering water in the lower pan. Whisk constantly until thickened, 5–10 minutes. Stir in the butter, mandarin orange zest, and liqueur. Remove from the heat, cover, and refrigerate for at least 3 hours or for up to 2 days.

On a lightly floured work surface, roll out the pastry into a round about 12 inches (30 cm) in diameter. Drape the pastry round over the rolling pin and carefully transfer it to a 9-inch (23-cm) tart pan with a removable bottom. Gently ease the pastry into the pan and trim the edges even with the pan rim. Place in the freezer for 30 minutes or for as long as overnight. Fully bake the pie shell as directed on page 13. Remove from the oven, place on a rack, and let cool completely before filling.

Carefully remove the pan sides and slide the tart off the pan bottom onto a serving plate. Spoon the filling into the cooled tart shell.

To make the topping, in a bowl, using an electric mixer, whip the cream until soft peaks form. Beat in the confectioners' sugar, half of the mandarin orange zest, and liqueur. Spread the cream over the top of the tart almost to the edges of the pastry. Garnish with the remaining mandarin orange zest and serve.

Serves 8

Pears Poached in Red Wine

juice of 1 lemon

6 small, firm but ripe Bosc, Winter Nellis, or Bartlett (Williams') pears

grated zest of 1 lemon and 1 orange

1 cinnamon stick

1 star anise

3 whole cloves

1 cup (8 oz/250 g) sugar

3 cups (24 fl oz/750 ml) dry red wine

½ cup (4 fl oz/125 ml) water

These pears are good on their own or topped with softly whipped cream. Try the recipe with apples, too.

✳

*H*ave ready a large bowl three-fourths full of water to which you have added the lemon juice. Peel the pears. Using a corer and starting at the bottom, remove the core from each pear to within about ½ inch (12 mm) of the stem. As each pear is peeled and cored, slip it into the lemon water to cover. (Alternatively, cut the pears in half lengthwise and remove the core.)

In a large saucepan over high heat, combine the lemon and orange zests, cinnamon, star anise, cloves, sugar, wine, and water; bring to a boil. Add the pears, reduce the heat to low, and poach, uncovered, until a skewer penetrates a pear easily, about 35 minutes (or 25 minutes for pear halves). Using a slotted spoon, transfer the pears to a bowl. Let the poaching liquid cool. Holding a fine-mesh sieve over the pears, strain the liquid through the sieve. Cover and refrigerate overnight or for up to 2 days.

To serve, bring to room temperature or warm slightly over low heat. Serve in individual bowls with a little of the poaching liquid.

Serves 6

Citrus and Honey Cheesecake with Nut Crust

Use dark honey for a fuller-bodied, more intense flavor. The cheesecake is best served slightly warm or at room temperature.

❀

For the crust:

2⅓ cups (12 oz/375 g) hazelnuts (filberts), toasted and skinned (*see glossary, page 107*)

⅓ cup (3 oz/90 g) sugar

½ teaspoon ground cinnamon

4–5 tablespoons (2–2½ oz/60–75 g) unsalted butter, melted

For the cheese filling:

1½ lb (750 g) cream cheese, at room temperature

½ cup (4 fl oz/125 ml) sour cream, at room temperature

¾ cup (9 oz/280 g) full-flavored honey

6 eggs, separated, at room temperature

1 tablespoon grated lemon zest

1 tablespoon grated orange zest

1 teaspoon vanilla extract (essence)

3 tablespoons chopped candied orange peel (optional)

¼ cup (2 oz/60 g) sugar

2 cups (8 oz/250 g) strawberries, stems removed (optional)

To make the crust, in a food processor, combine 2 cups (10 oz/315 g) of the hazelnuts with the sugar and the cinnamon. Process to chop as finely as possible; do not process to a paste. Transfer to a small bowl and stir in enough of the melted butter for the mixture to hold together in clumps. Press the mixture into the bottom and partially up the sides of a 9-inch (23-cm) springform pan. Set aside.

Preheat an oven to 350°F (180°C).

To make the filling, in a bowl, using an electric mixer set on high speed, beat together the cream cheese and sour cream until smooth. Add the honey and beat until no lumps remain. Add the egg yolks, lemon and orange zests, vanilla, and the candied orange peel, if using; mix well.

In a large bowl, beat the egg whites until frothy. Gradually beat in the sugar until the peaks are almost stiff. Stir one-third of the egg whites into the cheese mixture to lighten it, then fold in the remaining egg whites just until no white streaks remain. Pour into the prepared pan.

Bake until set just on the edges, 45–50 minutes; gently shake the pan to test. Turn off the oven, prop the door open, and leave the cheesecake inside for 2 hours.

Release and remove the sides from the pan and slide the cheesecake onto a serving plate. Chop the remaining ⅓ cup (2 oz/60 g) hazelnuts and scatter over the top. Surround the base with the berries, if desired, and serve.

Serves 8–10

Chocolate Pound Cake

1½ cups (7½ oz/235 g) all-purpose (plain) flour, sifted
½ cup (1½ oz/45 g) unsweetened Dutch-process cocoa powder, sifted
¼ teaspoon salt
2 oz (60 g) semisweet (plain) chocolate
1 cup (8 oz/250 g) unsalted butter, at room temperature
2 cups (14 oz/440 g) firmly packed light brown sugar
3 eggs
1 teaspoon vanilla extract (essence)
1 cup (8 oz/250 g) sour cream

Dust the pound cake with confectioners' (icing) sugar, if you wish. Slice and serve plain or topped with whipped cream or ice cream.

❊

Preheat an oven to 350°F (180°C). Butter a 9-by-5-inch (23-by-13-cm) loaf pan. In a bowl, sift together the sifted flour, sifted cocoa, and the salt. Set aside. Place the chocolate in the top pan of a double boiler or a heatproof bowl. Place over (not touching) simmering water in the lower pan and heat until melted, stirring until smooth.

Meanwhile, in a large bowl, using an electric mixer set on medium speed, beat together the butter and brown sugar until light and fluffy. Beat in the eggs, one at a time. Add the vanilla and the melted chocolate and mix well. Using a rubber spatula, fold the flour mixture into the butter mixture in 3 batches alternating with the sour cream and beginning and ending with the flour mixture. Pour the batter into the prepared loaf pan.

Bake until a toothpick inserted into the center of the cake comes out clean, about 1 hour. If the cake is browning too quickly, cover it loosely with aluminum foil. Remove the cake from the oven, place on a rack, and let cool for 10 minutes. Then turn out onto the rack and let cool completely. Cut into slices to serve.

Serves 6–8

Apple Charlotte

FOR THE CHARLOTTE:

12 McIntosh, Empire, or Rome Beauty
    apples, peeled, cored, and cubed
12 tablespoons (6 oz/185 g) unsalted
    butter, melted
¾ cup (6 oz/185 g) granulated sugar
½ teaspoon ground cinnamon
1 tablespoon grated lemon zest
1 teaspoon vanilla extract (essence)
12–15 slices white bread, each about
    ¼ inch (6 mm) thick, crusts removed

FOR THE BRANDIED WHIPPED CREAM:

1 cup (8 fl oz/250 ml) heavy (double)
    cream
¼ cup (1½ oz/45 g) confectioners' (icing)
    sugar, sifted
3 tablespoons brandy (optional)

FOR THE APRICOT SAUCE:

1 cup (10 oz/315 g) apricot jam
¼ cup (2 fl oz/60 ml) water
¼ cup (2 fl oz/60 ml) brandy (optional)

apricot halves and orange zest strips
    (optional)

*P*osition a rack in the lower third of an oven and preheat to 425°F (220°C).

To make the charlotte, in a large, heavy sauté pan over medium heat, combine the apples with 2 tablespoons of the melted butter. Cook, stirring occasionally, until the apples begin to soften, about 5 minutes. Add the granulated sugar, cinnamon, and lemon zest and stir to mix well. Continue to cook, stirring occasionally, until the apples break down into a very thick purée, about 15 minutes. Stir in the vanilla. If the apples are very tart, add a bit more sugar. You should have 5–6 cups (40–48 fl oz/1.25–1.5 l) apple purée.

Line the bottom and sides of a 6-cup (48–fl oz/1.5-l) round charlotte mold or soufflé dish with the bread slices without overlapping, cutting them into pieces as needed. Remove them, dip them in the remaining melted butter, and then again line the mold or dish with them. Spoon in the apple mixture and top with the remaining bread, dipping it first in the butter.

Bake for 10 minutes. Reduce the oven temperature to 350°F (180°C) and continue to bake until golden, about 30 minutes longer. Transfer to a rack. Let stand for 30 minutes, then invert the charlotte onto a serving plate and lift off the mold or dish.

Meanwhile, make the whipped cream: In a bowl, using an electric mixer or a whisk, beat together the cream and confectioners' sugar until soft peaks form. Cover and refrigerate until serving. Fold in the brandy, if desired.

To make the apricot sauce, in a small saucepan over low heat, stir together the jam and water until the jam melts and a sauce forms. Stir in the brandy, if desired.

To serve, top the warm charlotte with some of the whipped cream and serve the apricot sauce on the side. Garnish with apricot halves and orange zest, if desired.

Serves 6–8

Blood Orange Crème Brûlée

1 cup (8 fl oz/250 ml) blood orange juice or regular orange juice

½ cup (4 fl oz/125 ml) Grand Marnier or other orange-flavored liqueur

2 cups (16 fl oz/500 ml) heavy (double) cream

grated zest of 2 blood oranges or regular oranges

6 tablespoons (3 oz/90 g) plus ½ cup (4 oz/125 g) sugar

6 egg yolks, beaten

Blood oranges give this extra-rich dessert a vibrant color. You can make the custard up to 8 hours ahead, waiting until moments just before serving to caramelize the sugar topping.

❅

*I*n a small saucepan over high heat, combine the orange juice and liqueur. Bring to a boil and cook until reduced to ½ cup (4 fl oz/125 ml). Set aside. In another small saucepan over medium heat, stir together the cream, orange zest, and the 6 tablespoons sugar. Bring to a simmer, stirring constantly. Remove from the heat, cover, and let stand for 30 minutes.

Preheat an oven to 300°F (150°C).

Place the egg yolks in a bowl and stir in the cream mixture. Add the orange juice–liqueur mixture. Pour the mixture into six ¾-cup (6-fl oz/180-ml) ramekins, dividing it evenly. Place in a baking pan and pour hot water into the baking pan to come halfway up the sides of the ramekins. Bake until just set, 45–60 minutes. Remove from the oven and remove the ramekins from the baking pan. Place them in the refrigerator until cold, then cover and chill thoroughly, about 2 hours.

Preheat a broiler (griller). Sprinkle the remaining ½ cup (4 oz/125 g) sugar over the chilled custards. Slip under the broiler as close as possible to the heat source and broil (grill) until the sugar caramelizes, 3–4 minutes. Remove from the broiler and let stand until the melted sugar hardens, then serve.

Serves 6

Ginger Florentines

4 tablespoons (2 oz/60 g) unsalted butter

1½ cups (6 oz/185 g) sliced (flaked) almonds

½ cup (4 oz/125 g) sugar

⅓ cup (3 fl oz/80 ml) heavy (double) cream

¼ cup (3 oz/90 g) honey

¼ cup (1½ oz/45 g) chopped candied orange peel

¼ cup (1½ oz/45 g) chopped crystallized ginger

½ teaspoon vanilla extract (essence)

¼ teaspoon ground cinnamon

¼ cup (1½ oz/45 g) all-purpose (plain) flour

4 oz (125 g) semisweet (plain) chocolate

Candied ginger adds an exotic flair to these crisp-textured, lacy cookies. Serve them on their own or as an accompaniment to Blood Orange Crème Brûlée (page 100).

❈

Preheat an oven to 325°F (165°C).

In a small saucepan over low heat, melt 2 tablespoons of the butter. Remove from the heat. Line the bottom of 2 baking sheets with parchment (baking) paper and brush the paper with the melted butter.

Chop 1 cup (4 oz/125 g) of the almonds. In a food processor or blender, place the remaining ½ cup (2 oz/60 g) almonds. Pulse until finely chopped; be careful not to pulse to a paste.

In a small, deep saucepan over low heat, combine the sugar, cream, honey, and the remaining 2 tablespoons butter. Stir to dissolve the sugar. Then raise the heat to medium, bring to a boil, and cook until a candy thermometer registers 238°F (114°C). Stir in the candied orange peel, crystallized ginger, vanilla, cinnamon, flour, and both the chopped and finely chopped almonds. Remove from the heat and let cool.

Drop the mixture by the teaspoonful onto the baking sheets, spacing the cookies 3 inches (7.5 cm) apart. Spread the mixture into flat rounds with the back of a spoon. You should have 24 rounds.

Bake until golden brown, about 12 minutes. Remove from the oven and let cool on the baking sheets for several minutes. Then, using a spatula, transfer to racks and let cool completely.

Meanwhile, place the chocolate in the top pan of a double boiler or in a heatproof bowl. Place over (not touching) simmering water in the lower pan. Heat until melted, stirring until smooth. Coat one side of each of 12 cookies with chocolate and top with a second cookie. Let stand until set, then serve.

Makes 12 cookies

Glossary

The following glossary defines terms specifically as they relate to festive entertaining. Included are major and unusual ingredients and basic techniques.

ANCHOVIES
Tiny saltwater fish common throughout the Mediterranean. Imported anchovy fillets packed in olive oil are widely available, while those packed in salt, sold in Italian delicatessens, are considered the finest.

BELGIAN ENDIVE
Leaf vegetable with refreshing, slightly bitter, spear-shaped leaves, white to pale yellow-green—or sometimes red—in color and tightly packed in cylindrical heads 4–6 inches (10–15 cm) long. The leaves can be used in salads and are perfectly shaped to hold fillings. Also known as witloof and chicory.

BELL PEPPERS
Sweet-fleshed, bell-shaped members of the pepper family; also known as capsicums. Most commonly sold in the unripe green form, although ripened red or yellow varieties are also available.

To roast bell peppers, preheat a broiler (griller). Cut the peppers in half lengthwise, then remove the stems, seeds, and any thin white membrane, or ribs. Place the halves, cut sides down, on a broiler pan and broil (grill) until the skins blister and blacken. Remove from the broiler, cover loosely with aluminum foil, and let stand until cool enough to handle, about 10 minutes. Using your fingertips or a small knife, peel off the blackened skins, then cut the peppers as directed in the individual recipes.

BLACK OLIVE PASTE
Thick, dark paste made from ripe olives and oil. Available in specialty-food shops and Italian delicatessens, black olive paste lends an intense flavor to a variety of Mediterranean dishes, especially fillings, dips, rubs, and sauces.

CALVADOS
A dry French brandy distilled from apples and bearing the fruit's distinctive aroma and taste. Dry applejack may be substituted.

CANDIED ORANGE PEEL
Made by saturating pieces of orange peel in sugar syrup and then drying them. Often sold chopped, candied orange peel is also available cut into narrow strips. Both forms are used to flavor and garnish desserts.

CHEESE
Cheeses made from the milk of goats, cows, or sheep are staples of the well-stocked kitchen. They make an excellent ingredient in or garnish for festive dishes.

Emmentaler Variety of Swiss cheese with a firm, smooth texture, large holes, and a mellow, slightly sweet, nutty flavor.

Feta White, salty, sharp-tasting cheese, with a crumbly, somewhat creamy consistency. Made from the milk of goats, sheep, or cows.

Goat Cheese Usually sold shaped into small rounds or logs, most goat cheeses are fresh and creamy, with a distinctively sharp tang. Some, however, are aged a bit longer and are then firmer in texture and sharper in taste. Also called by the French term *chèvre*.

Gruyère Variety of Swiss cheese with a firm, smooth texture, small holes, and a strong, tangy flavor.

Monterey Jack Cow's milk cheese widely available in two forms: unaged jack is butter colored, semisoft, and mild in flavor, while aged or dry jack is darker, firm textured, and sharp in flavor.

Parmesan Hard, thick-crusted Italian cow's milk cheese with a sharp, salty, full flavor resulting from at least 2 years of aging. The finest Italian variety is designated Parmigiano-Reggiano®. Buy in block form, to shave or grate fresh as needed.

Roquefort French blue-veined cheese made from sheep's milk, with a creamy texture and a rich, sharply tangy flavor. Other creamy blue-veined cheeses can be substituted.

CHOCOLATE
Use the finest quality chocolate available for the best results. Two kinds of chocolate are used in this book. Semisweet chocolate is an eating or a cooking chocolate enriched with cocoa butter and sweetened with sugar. It should contain at least 15 percent chocolate liquor, although the percentage may vary. Unsweetened cocoa is a fine-textured powder ground from solid chocolate liquor. Cocoa specially treated to reduce its natural acidity, resulting in a darker color and more mellow flavor, is known as Dutch-process cocoa.

CIPOLLINE
These small, flat, brown-skinned onions are prized for their sweetness; available in well-stocked vegetable markets.

COCONUT MILK
Although often mistakenly thought to be the liquid found inside whole coconuts, coconut milk, which imparts a richness to sweet and savory dishes, is actually made by steeping shredded fresh coconut in an equal amount of boiling water. It can also be purchased in cans in Asian markets and well-stocked food stores. Do not confuse coconut milk with coconut cream, its richer, thicker relative.

CORNISH HEN
A cross between Cornish and White Rock chickens, the Cornish hen commonly weighs about 1½ pounds (750 g), which is small enough to be a single serving.

COUSCOUS
Originating in North Africa, these small, granular beads of semolina develop a fluffy consistency when cooked. Authentic couscous can take

CITRUS FRUITS

A wide variety of citrus fruits, from the common lemon to the exotic blood orange, enlivens festive dishes, both savory and sweet. The colorful zest, the flesh, and the juice of citrus fruits are all used in recipes.

Blood Orange   Orange with reddish flesh and juice and red-blushed orange skin. The flavor is more pronounced than that of regular oranges and the color adds a festive touch to salads and desserts. Regular oranges can be substituted.

Grapefruit   Pink- and red-fleshed grapefruits are available year-round and vary in flavor from sweet to tart. Cut into segments, they add sparkle and tang to green salads. Grapefruit juice is used in vinaigrettes and other sauces.

Lemon   Available year-round, fresh lemons are tart and full of flavor. The zest and juice of the lemon are more often used than its flesh. The juicy, gold-tinged flesh of the Meyer variety, however, is sweet enough to eat.

Mandarin Orange   Easy to peel but usually containing many seeds. Mandarins vary in flavor from sweet to tart, depending upon type. Among the many varieties available are the really seedless, sweet satsuma and the sweet-tart clementine. Mandarins can be used in place of oranges for zest, flesh, or juice. Also known as tangerines.

The zest, the brightly colored, outermost layer of a citrus fruit's peel, contains most of the fruit's flavorful oils. Zest may be removed using one of two easy methods.

Use a simple tool known as a zester, drawing its sharp-edged holes across the fruit's skin to remove the zest in thin strips, or use the fine holes on a handheld grater.

Alternatively, cut off the zest in thin strips with a vegetable peeler or paring knife, taking care not to remove any white pith with it. Then thinly slice or chop on a cutting board.

Some recipes call for segments, or sections, of citrus fruits, free of pith and membranes.

To section a citrus fruit, using a small knife, cut a thick slice off the bottom and top to expose the fruit. Then, steadying the fruit upright on a cutting board, thickly slice off the peel in strips, cutting around the contour of the fruit to expose the flesh.

Holding the peeled fruit over a bowl, cut along either side of each section, letting the sections drop into the bowl. Remove any seeds and discard.

---

close to an hour to cook, but many food stores sell an acceptable instant variety that has been precooked and then redried. Couscous makes an excellent bed for grilled or stewed vegetables, fish, poultry, and meats.

FENNEL

Crisp, refreshing, mildly anise-flavored bulb vegetable, sometimes called by its Italian name, *finocchio*. Fennel can be served raw, in salads, or cooked. Small, dried, crescent-shaped fennel seeds are used as a spice in cooking and baking.

FIGS

Late summer and early autumn fruits characterized by their many tiny edible seeds, sweet and sometimes nutty flavor, and soft, tender texture. Figs are available fresh and dried; when buying fresh figs, select ones that are fully ripe and use them immediately.

FILO

Tissue-thin sheets of flour-and-water pastry usually found in the freezer case of a food market or purchased fresh in Greek and Middle Eastern delicatessens. Defrost frozen filo in the refrigerator thoroughly before use. When working with filo, always keep the unused sheets covered with a lightly dampened kitchen towel to prevent them from drying out.

GRAPE LEAVES

In Greek and other Middle Eastern cuisines, the leaves of the grapevine are commonly used as edible wrappers. If using fresh leaves, wash thoroughly before use, then blanch or steam briefly until pliable.

Bottled leaves, available in Greek and Italian delicatessens and the specialty-food section of well-stocked food markets, should be gently rinsed of their brine.

LENTILS, GREEN

This popular variety of the small, disk-shaped dried legume makes a delicate side dish or salad. The most prized green lentil comes from Le Puy, France. When preparing any lentils, always pick through them carefully before cooking to remove stones, fibers, misshapen beans, or other impurities. Unlike other dried legumes, lentils do not need to be soaked before cooking.

HERBS

All manner of herbs, both fresh and dried, serve as seasonings and garnishes. Among the most common types used in this book are

Basil Sweet, spicy herb popular in Italian and French cooking, particularly as a seasoning for tomatoes.

Bay Leaves Dried whole leaves of the bay laurel tree. Pungent and spicy, they flavor stocks and other simmered dishes. The French variety has a milder, sweeter flavor than California bay leaves.

Chives Mild, sweet herb with a fine, grasslike appearance and the subtle flavor of onion, to which it is related.

Cilantro Green, leafy herb resembling flat-leaf (Italian) parsley, with a sharp, somewhat astringent flavor. Also known as coriander or Chinese parsley.

Dill Herb with fine, feathery leaves and a sweet, aromatic flavor that complements vegetable dishes.

Mint Refreshing sweet herb used fresh to season or garnish salads, soups, vegetables, and grain dishes.

Oregano Aromatic, pungent, and spicy herb—also known as wild marjoram—used fresh or dried as a seasoning for all kinds of savory dishes, especially tomatoes and other vegetables.

Parsley A popular herb available in two main varieties, the more popular curly-leaf type and a flat-leaf parsley. The latter, also known as Italian parsley, is preferred for its pronounced flavor. Both are available fresh in well-stocked food stores and vegetable markets. Also used dried.

Rosemary A member of the mint family with needle-like leaves and a strong, aromatic flavor, well suited to use with poultry, lamb, and pork. Used fresh or dried.

Sage Pungent, slightly bitter herb used fresh or dried; complements vegetables, poultry, pork, and lamb.

Summer Savory Aromatic and sweet herb used fresh and dried to season vegetables and poultry.

Tarragon Fragrant, distinctively sweet herb used fresh or dried as a seasoning for chicken and light meats, seafood, and eggs.

Thyme Minty, small-leaved herb. A variety called lemon thyme has a subtle lemon scent and taste.

LOBSTER

Firm-fleshed shellfish with a rich, sweet flavor. Lobster is a special ingredient, well suited to festive entertaining. For the freshest and best-tasting lobster meat for salads, buy a live lobster and cook it yourself.

Once the lobster is cooked as specified in the recipe, let it rest until cool enough to handle. Then, steadying the body with one hand, firmly grasp a claw where it joins the body; twist and pull to remove it. Repeat with the other claw.

To extract the meat from the claw, crack its shell with a lobster cracker or mallet. Peel away the shell and remove the meat, taking care to keep it in one piece if possible. Twist and pull

off the four small legs arrayed along each side of the body.

To split the lobster in half, turn it underside up on the work surface. Steadying it with one hand, use a large, sharp knife to cut through the soft shell from head to tail.

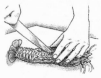

Continue cutting through the head and tail sections and downward through the shell along the back. If a black vein is visible along the center of the tail meat, remove it and discard.

Using a small spoon, scoop out the stomach sac and other soft matter from the head portion of the shell halves. Using a fork, spear one end of the tail meat and gently pull it out of the shell. If the recipe requires the shell halves for presentation, clean and reserve them.

MUSHROOMS

With their meaty texture and rich, earthy flavor, mushrooms add a touch of luxury to many festive meals. Common, deep-capped white and brown mushrooms can be stuffed with many flavorful fillings such as sausage and herbs, and served as a starter, while more exotic varieties should be shown off either on their own or mixed with other vegetables and served as a side dish. Among these more exotic types are chanterelles, which are subtly flavored, pale yellow, trumpet-shaped wild mushrooms 2–3 inches (5–7.5 cm) in length. They are also cultivated commercially and may be found in well-stocked food stores and vegetable markets.

NUTS

Rich and mellow in flavor, crisp and crunchy in texture, a wide variety of nuts is used throughout the recipes in this book, both savory and sweet. *Almonds,* oval in shape, have a mellow, sweet flavor.

They are sold whole with their skins intact, or blanched (with their skins removed), slivered, or thinly sliced (flaked). *Walnuts* are rich, crisp nuts with distinctively crinkled surfaces. *Hazelnuts,* also known as filberts, are spherical and slightly sweet. *Pine nuts* are small ivory seeds extracted from the cones of a species of pine tree. They possess a rich, subtly resinous flavor. Toasting nuts, whether whole, chopped, or sliced, develops their rich flavor and helps to keep them crisp.

To toast nuts, preheat an oven to 325°F (165°C). Spread the nuts in a single layer on a rimmed baking sheet and toast in the oven until just beginning to color, 5–10 minutes. Remove from the oven and let cool to room temperature.

Toasting also loosens the skins of hazelnuts and walnuts, which may be removed by wrapping the still-warm nuts in a kitchen towel and rubbing against them with the palms of your hands.

PARSNIPS

Root vegetable similar in shape and texture to a carrot but with ivory flesh and an appealingly sweet flavor. Widely available in the cooler months, parsnips work well in combination with other root vegetables, both roasted and mashed.

PLUMS, ITALIAN PRUNE

Oval and pleasantly tart-sweet, Italian prune plums are a good choice for baking because their flesh tends to be slightly dry and their pits are easy to remove. They are also delicious eaten out of hand.

POUSSIN

Small, immature chicken, weighing no more than about 1 pound (500 g), prized for its tender, sweet flesh. Each bird yields a single serving.

PROSCIUTTO

Italian-style ham, cured by dry-salting for 1 month, followed by cool-air drying for 6 months or more. An expensive ingredient, prosciutto is usually treated simply in cooking, in order not to obscure its fine slightly sweet, mildly salty flavor. A specialty of Parma, Italy.

SARDINES

Small fish popular throughout the Mediterranean. A bit bigger than the anchovy, the sardine, a relative of the herring, is available fresh or canned in oil. Like anchovies, sardines can be mashed to flavor fillings and sauces. Fresh sardines are excellent grilled.

SEEDS

Seeds such as sesame and fennel can be used whole as a coating or crust, or ground and mixed into a dish for more subtle flavor. Toasting seeds before use heightens and releases their flavor.

To toast seeds, place them in a small, dry heavy frying pan over medium heat and stir until aromatic and beginning to color, 1–2 minutes. If grinding is required, let cool slightly, then place in an electric spice mill or a clean coffee grinder and pulverize, or crush them in a mortar with a pestle.

SHRIMP

Raw shrimp (prawns) are usually sold with their heads already removed but their shells intact. They may be peeled and their thin, veinlike intestinal tracts removed before cooking.

To peel, using your thumbs, split open the shrimp's thin shell along the concave side, between its two rows of legs. Peel away the shell; leave the last segment with tail fin intact and attached to the meat, if desired. Using a small, sharp knife, carefully make a shallow slit along the peeled shrimp's back, just deep enough to expose the long, usually dark, veinlike intestinal tract.

With the tip of the knife or your fingers, lift up and pull out the vein, discarding it.

STAR ANISE

A star-shaped seedpod, similar in flavor to aniseed. Asian in origin, star anise is one of the ingredients used to make Chinese five-spice powder. Used whole, it imparts flavor to poaching liquids, stocks, and sauces.

TOMATOES

When tomatoes are in season, use the best sun-ripened tomatoes you can find. At other times of year, plum tomatoes, sometimes called Roma or egg tomatoes, are likely to have the best flavor and texture.

To peel fresh tomatoes, bring a saucepan of water to a boil. Meanwhile, using a small sharp knife, cut out the core from the stem end of the tomato, then cut a shallow X in the skin at the tomato's base. Immerse in the boiling water for about 20 seconds, then remove and slip into a bowl of cold water to cool. Lift out and, starting at the X, peel the skin from the tomato, using your fingertips and, if necessary, the knife.

Cut the tomato in half and turn each half cut side down. Cut as directed in individual recipes.

To seed a tomato, cut in half crosswise. Squeeze gently to force out the seed sacs.

Index

Acknowledgments

The following authors provided the recipes for this book: Joyce Goldstein: pages 10, 11, 13, 16, 18, 25, 28, 31, 33, 34, 37, 38, 41,
42, 45, 46, 49, 51, 52, 54, 67, 68, 74, 78, 80, 83, 84, 86, 89, 91, 92, 95, 96, 99, 100, 102; Chuck Williams: pages 57, 58, 61, 65, 73, 77;
Scotto Sisters: pages 12, 15, 21, 22, 27; John Phillip Carroll: page 63; and Jacqueline Mallorca: page 71.
The publishers thank the following people for their generous assistance and support in producing this book:
Desne Border, Ken DellaPenta, Julia Schlosser, Karen Nicks, Danielle Di Salvo, and Janice Baker. The following kindly lent props for the
photography: Williams-Sonoma, Pottery Barn, Chuck Williams, Sue Fisher King, Biordi Art Imports, and Fillamento. The publishers also
thank all the other individuals and organizations that provided props, locations, and other assistance in producing this book.